GREEN MALAYSIA

RAINFOREST ENCOUNTERS

EDITORIAL BOARD	Cheah Kam Huan
	Michael Rajoo
	Suria Zainal
	Aimi Lee Abdullah
AUTHOR	Premilla Mohanlall
TECHNICAL ADVISORS	Thang Hooi Chiew
	Dr Halijah Ibrahim
	Shaharuddin bin Mohamad Ismail
	Dr Yong Hoi Sen
PHOTOGRAPHY	EDM Archives
	MTC Image Bank
	Terry Ong
	Picture Library
	Worldwide Fund for Nature, Malaysia
ILLUSTRATORS	Yeap Kok Chien
	Sui Chen Choi
	Tang Hong Yew
	Chai Kah Yune
EDITOR	Dianne Buerger
DESIGNERS	Lee King Hon
	Theivanai A/P Nadaraju
PRODUCTION MANAGER	Sin Kam Cheong

Acknowledgments: Thank you to Dewan Bahasa dan Pustaka, Forest Research Institute Malaysia, Forestry Department Peninsular Malaysia, Forestry Department Sabah, Forestry Department Sarawak, Malaysia Airports Berhad, Malaysian Branch of the Royal Asiatic Society, Malaysian Wetlands Foundation, Pepper Marketing Board Malaysia, Sabah Adventure Rally, Sarawak Tourism Board and Tanjong Jara Resort.

Designed and produced by
EDITIONS DIDIER MILLET SDN BHD
25 Jalan Pudu Lama
50200 Kuala Lumpur, Malaysia
www.edmbooks.com

ISBN 981-4068-53-5

Photographs on pp. 1–8

p. 1: Massive dipterocarp buttresses; p. 4: Virgin jungle at Sungei Belawan, c. 1907; p. 6: Stream in Malaysian rainforest;
pp. 8–9: Aerial view of the Malaysian tropical rainforest.

GREEN MALAYSIA

RAINFOREST ENCOUNTERS

MALAYSIAN TIMBER COUNCIL

CONTENTS

F O R E W O R D

With over one hundred years of forest management, Malaysia's forest heritage is something that all Malaysians should be proud of. *Green Malaysia: Rainforest Encounters* is a fascinating journey into the mysterious and enchanting world of the Malaysian rainforest, and invites the reader to glimpse into its past, present and into what lies ahead.

Green Malaysia: Rainforest Encounters is testament to the fact that Malaysia has not only espoused, but also practised the concept of sustainable development. Economic gain is often perceived as being at odds with the need to conserve the environment. However, since 1901, the Government has made a determined effort to ensure that these natural resources are not harvested at the expense of the environment. In reality, proper management requires substantial financing, and the irony of calls to preserve the forests *in toto* lies in the fact that such funds are generated mainly through the commercial utilization of forest resources. The forest itself is a living entity that keeps changing, requiring reviews and improvements of management practices every now and again. Striking such a fine balance is not easy, since idealism and economic practicality have never been the best of friends.

Produced in commemoration of the Malaysian Timber Council's tenth anniversary, this book aims at enhancing the reader's understanding of the multifarious dynamics within a tropical rainforest such as Malaysia's. It also highlights Malaysia's stance on environmental and forestry issues in international fora. In the process, we hope that it will enlighten the reader on the basic tenets of sustainable forest management and the complications and expense involved in its implementation.

With extensive research, excellent photography and beautiful artwork, we hope that *Green Malaysia: Rainforest Encounters* will be a source of reference for students, laymen and those who wish to gain an insight into the mystery of Malaysia's green jewel. It is a project that we are highly passionate about, and we hope you enjoy the book as much as we have taken pleasure in producing it. It is also a tribute to all those involved in managing the country's forest resources for our children and future generations.

This book celebrates everything about the Malaysian rainforest: its intricate ecosystem, dynamism and various life forms in a multitude of colours, smells and appearances. But above all, it is a tribute to Mother Nature who has endowed us with such a wonderful piece of green heritage with all its beauty, diversity, wealth and mystery.

DATO' ISMAIL AWANG
Chief Executive Officer

CHAPTER ONE

THE WORLD'S FORESTS

The map of the world today consists predominantly of splashes of green, brown and blue. Green defines the forests that grow between vast expanses of barren, brown deserts, which together rise above the vast blue oceans of the Pacific, Atlantic, Indian and Arctic. Together, they support an estimated five to 100 million species of living organisms in a delicately balanced web of life. The green cover of forest occupies less than 30 per cent of the earth's surface, straddling across the globe in one discontinuous sweep. World vegetation maps tend to divide the globe into three vegetation zones—tropical, temperate and boreal—each with its own 'signature' forest, determined by variables such as climate, sunlight, rainfall, soil conditions and elevation.

Tropical rainforests, near the hot and moist Equatorial zone, have captured the imagination of the world as dark and brooding keepers of the planet's secrets. They occupy a mere seven per cent of the land surface, but their elaborate architecture contains extraordinarily rich and fragile habitats that house more than 50 per cent of the species in the entire world biota. Well over half the rainforests of the world occur in South America, almost one-fifth in Africa and more than one quarter in Southeast Asia. Characterized by an abundance of profuse, tangled, climbing and entwined vegetation, all these rainforests share a common geological history. The continents of Africa, South America and Southeast Asia once belonged to the massive landmass called Gondwanaland, which was shattered by the Earth heaving sighs of seismic activity or drowned with the onslaught of melting ice sheets. Flora and fauna that evolved on Gondwanaland adapted to new geological developments, topography and climate and began to have their own respective identities. Rainforests in Southeast Asia are for the most part, evergreen, with no single dominant species; while African rainforests are predominantly semi-evergreen, with the domination of one or a few tree species and South American rainforests are made up of evergreen, semi-evergreen and deciduous species.

Temperate forests take shape in the higher latitudes, which enjoy warm moist summers and cold, sometimes harsh, snowy winters in the higher ranges. The growing season sprawls over a period of six months. Throughout spring and summer broadleaf

The carnivorous *Nepenthes* or pitcher plant grows wild in nutrient-poor soils.

OPPOSITE: Beneath the massive canopy of giant tropical rainforest trees lies an intricate web of plant and animal life.

deciduous staples such as oak, maple, beech, chestnut, hickory, elm and dogwood are nurtured. Most temperate broadleaf forests are dominated by a few species of trees, which are used to label the forest; hence, beech-maple forest or oak-hickory forests.

The parade of seasons is vividly expressed in temperate deciduous forests, which go through the rites of spring, summer, autumn and winter. Attractive maples, beeches and birches are the temperate forest beauties, seen in full glory with their impressive display of colour in autumn, when their leaves turn from green to yellow and from gold to red before browning and falling to the ground. Surprisingly, the tallest trees in the world do not belong to the realms of the rainforest; they are the handsome California redwoods, once common throughout the Northern hemisphere but now found exclusively on the Pacific Coast of North America. The official tree of the state of California, they are also national treasures preserved in state and national parks and forests. There are two species of the California redwood: the coast redwood (*Sequoia sempervirens*) and the giant sequoia (*Sequoiadendron giganteum*). Temperate forests also contain pockets of conifers, mostly pine, where soils are poor and temperatures colder. In some warmer and moister pockets, temperate rainforests thrive. Here are found the Sitka spruce, Western hemlock, Western red cedar and Douglas-fir, believed to be remnants of giant coniferous forests that once covered a much greater part of the earth millions of years ago.

The boreal forest is the land of Christmas trees, where giant conifers such as the spruce, pine and fir stand tall, undeterred by the winter winds and heavy snows that befall them in the colder northern latitudes of North America, Europe and Asia. These statuesque glacial beauties can withstand the harsh northern winters. Their needle-like leaves are arranged to shed snow and block wind. Their waxy coating helps prevent water loss and contains a thick sap that prevents them from freezing in winter. Not surprisingly, boreal forests have low biodiversity, with vast tracts of land dominated by a single species of trees. The coniferous sentinels of the boreal forest gradually degenerate into patches of small, scraggly trees, and eventually disappear in the open tundra.

All forests are dynamic environments which, once established, are hardy, self-renewing machines. While nourishing themselves, they also share their bounties with other life forms, feeding and fertilizing them in a manner befitting their status as Mother Nature. The leaves capture the sun's energy, and through photosynthesis, convert water and carbon dioxide to produce carbohydrates, the sustenance for many living things, large and small. During this activity, the forest releases oxygen and absorbs carbon dioxide. This function of the forest has received much attention from some environmentalists who regard forests as the primary agents of climate control, absorbing carbon dioxide emissions to help reduce air pollution and retard global warming.

A Petition from the Countryside

give us
  land
  from the jungle
the forest vines are finished
  they are covered in thorns
the forest creepers are finished
  eaten by pigs
the fish have vanished from the ponds
  swallowed by snakes.

give us
  a little land
  from this earth
we will turn
  the vines into rubber trees
  so that
  our children can wear shoes
we will turn
  the creepers into rice
  so that
  our children will not starve
we will turn
  the lakes into oceans
  so that
  our children have strong bodies.

MOECHTAR AWANG

WORLD FOREST TYPES

Ice cap

North Pole
1. Tundra
2. Cold temperate
3. Warm temperate
4. Desert
5. Savannah
6. Tropical rainforest   Equator
Savannah
Desert
Warm temperate
Cold temperate
Ice cap
South Pole

Tropic of Cancer

Tropic of Capricorn

Northern Hemisphere

Southern Hemisphere

Enlarged area 1–6

WHAT IS A FOREST?

Forests are determined by the presence
of trees and the absence of other predominant
land uses. Forests include natural forests, forest
plantations, forests for purposes of production, protection,
multiple use or conservation (national parks, nature reserves
and other protected areas), as well as forest stands on agricultural
lands and rubberwood plantations and cork stands. The term 'forest'
excludes fruit tree plantations. *Source: FAO State of the World's Forests report (2001)*

1. Tundra

2. Cold temperate

3. Warm temperate

4. Desert

5. Savannah

6. Tropical rainforest

DISTRIBUTION OF TROPICAL RAINFORESTS

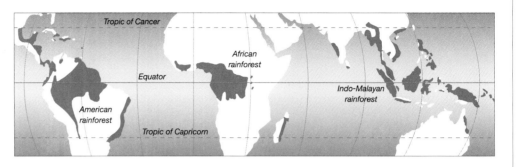

Environmental extremists have latched on to deforestation as one of the causes of reducing the earth's capacity to mitigate rising carbon dioxide emissions. Several studies, however, show that this argument is flawed. A team of scientists from Princeton University has shown that the burning of fossil fuels is a far greater generator of carbon dioxide emissions. In another study conducted in North Carolina, USA, researchers concluded that after the initial growth spurt trees grow more slowly and do not absorb as much excess carbon from the atmosphere as expected. Their findings show that existing forests cannot be counted on to eliminate the threat of global warming. While forests provide some relief, oceans are more effective as carbon sinks, absorbing almost two-thirds of carbon dioxide emissions.

Another forest function that has stirred strong reactions is the issue of biodiversity, especially in the species-rich tropical rainforest. From the 1980s onwards the spotlight shifted from the extrinsic to the intrinsic value of forests, centred mainly on biodiversity, which refers to the variety and variability of all animals, plants and microorganisms on earth. Some biodiversity is essential, as mankind is dependent on other species for the maintenance of the biosphere and the supply of basic necessities such as food. Even more important is the potential inherent in these species which have been described as the world's most fundamental capital stock. Forests, particularly rainforests, are regarded as awesome hypermarkets and pharmacies; almost half of today's main food crops were originally discovered in the rainforest, including bananas, mangoes, papayas, tea, sugar, rice, maize, nuts, cloves, vanilla, cinnamon, and coffee. Even the common domestic fowl originated in Indian forests.

The World Health Organization estimates that 80 per cent of the population in developing countries rely on traditional medicines (generally based on wild plants and animals) for their primary health

Medicinal plants such as *hempedu bumi* (*Andrographis paniculata)* are sought-after by the world's pharmaceutical industry.

care. There are more than 1,000 species of plants in Malaysia reported to have medicinal properties that are used for treating common ailments such as headaches, coughs and colds to dangerous tropical illnesses such as malaria and cholera. Breakthrough research has recently identified the wild *bintangor* tree (*Calophyllum lanigerum* var. *austrocoriaceum*), which grows in Malaysian forests as possibly holding the key to finding a cure for the devastating disease, AIDS.

Recent global surveys suggest that there are about 1.75 million documented species of plants and animals, though general consensus is that this is a conservative estimate. Analysts of the 2002 Global Environment Outlook-3 report by the United Nations Environment Programme say that its figures are in line with projections that 15–20 per cent of species diversity are under threat of extinction in the next 100 years. The main cause of loss of biological diversity is the loss of habitats, with forests being cleared for agriculture, habitation and fuel in developing countries struggling to make ends meet. Poverty eradication is thus seen as the solution to arrest the decline in forest species.

Forests also contribute to the national economy through tourism and export revenues. Tourism is not only a sustainable way to use the forest but also economically practical. Timber and wood products have a variety of uses for local communities and for export markets. With well-managed forests, the quality of life of plants, animals and humans—will not be compromised.

Man has an ambivalent relationship with the forest: he respects it, even eulogizes over it, but in the struggle for the survival of the species, he competes with it in his need for more space, food and shelter for his growing number. When economic necessity supersedes ecological considerations, the delicate balance of fragile ecosystems is jeopardized. Environmental degradation occurs, resulting in poor soil, pollution, ozone depletion and global warming that could culminate in the extinction of many species, including his own.

The relationship between economic development and environmental degradation was first placed on the international agenda in 1972, with the convening of the United Nations Conference on the Human Environment held in Stockholm, Sweden. By 1983, mounting concerns on global environmental stress resulted in the Brundtland Commission, which introduced the term

Forests have been cleared in developing and poverty-stricken countries to plant food crops and for commercial agricultural development.

TREE COVER IN MALAYSIA COMPARED TO SELECTED COUNTRIES

Climate is a key determinant in the extent of natural tree cover, which flourishes in the equatorial conditions of Malaysia–uniformly high temperatures, humidity and rainfall.

Tree cover (%)

Australia *(768.23)	France *(55.01)	Sweden *(41.16)	Germany *(34.93)	Malaysia *(32.83)	U.K. *(24.16)
20.1%	27.9%	65.9%	30.7%	77.6%	11.6%

*Total land area (million hectares)

Source: Fact Sheets Forestry and Environment: Malaysian Timber Council 2002

'sustainable development' as the alternative approach and resulted in a marriage of what had been hitherto assumed to be strange bedfellows: economic and social policies with environmental strategies. For the first time in 1992, more than 8,000 delegates including many world leaders and environmental groups from 180 countries arrived in Rio de Janeiro for the landmark Earth Summit organized by the United Nations Conference on Environment and Development (UNCED). This gave further impetus to the concept of sustainable development, where the need to balance a nation's economic imperatives while observing global rules in managing the environment was spelt out.

Issues such as global deforestation, loss of biological diversity, mitigation of climatic changes and environmental degradation were recognized as issues requiring immediate international remedial action. Rio produced five documents: a major action plan, two statements of principles and two international agreements. Essentially a blueprint to make human development socially, economically and environmentally sustainable, the action plan called Agenda 21 defined the rights and responsibilities of nations in their pursuit of human development. For the world forestry sector, a statement of principles was drafted to guide the management, conservation and sustainable development of all types of forests, which were recognized as being essential for economic development and the maintenance of all life forms. The agreements were negotiated separately but reflected the spirit of the Earth Summit. The United Nations Framework Convention on Climate Change (FCCC) sought to stabilize atmospheric greenhouse gases to avert global climatic disasters. The Convention on Biological Diversity requires signatories to adopt measures to conserve the variety of living species and ensure that the benefits of using biological diversity are equitably shared. Malaysia is a signatory to both the FCCC and the Convention on Biological Diversity.

Malaysia is signatory to treaties to preserve protected species such as the Malaysian tiger.

CITES

International trade in wildlife and wildlife products is regulated by the Convention on International Trade in Endangered Species of Wild Fauna and Flora (CITES), a 1975 treaty with 152 signatories.

CITES has caused considerable debate in recent years. In 1992, The Netherlands and Denmark proposed the listing of tropical timbers such as *ramin* (*Gonystylus bancanus*) and *merbau* (*Intsia palembanica*) as threatened species.

In 1994, non-producing countries used CITES to restrict timber exports of African mahogany (*Khaya ivorensis*), mahogany (*Swietenia macrophylla*) from South America and *ramin* from Indonesia and Malaysia. In both cases, the attempt failed because producing countries were able to present substantiated data proving that these species were not threatened. Eventually CITES ruled in their favour.

However, in 2001, Indonesia voluntarily listed *ramin* under Appendix III (species in which trade needs to meet certain permit requirements), due to rampant illegal logging and trade in *ramin*.

FUNCTIONS OF THE FOREST

Forests fulfil many functions: providing an arena of diversity for research, food and homes to animals, plants and humans. Forests provide a venue for recreation and are a source of livelihood through tourism, timber and other forest-related industries. Forests also contribute to climate and pollution control, prevent erosion and provide natural water catchment areas.

Timber and timber-based products are an important source of revenue for many forest-rich countries.

The forest provides a home to many animals, including the orang utan.

Isolated forest settlements usually rely on the bounty of the forest to survive.

Tropical rainforests are a haven for birds and bird-watchers.

Streams are natural water catchments and make idyllic picnic spots.

Cyclists and runners use old logging trails for recreation.

Tissue culture research is undertaken for forest species propagation.

Angling is a common recreational activity.

The mangrove forest is home to crabs, prawns and fish and is also a rich source of fuelwood.

Agricultural plantations are a source of revenue and employment in many countries.

Freshwater wetlands provide a habitat for flora and fauna to develop, help mitigate flooding, act as water catchment areas and help prevent the erosion of soil.

It has not been a smooth and easy road to implement all the principles set out in Agenda 21. Developed nations continue to play the tropical forestry card, pressuring Third World nations, where most of the tropical forests are located, to restrict their exports of forestry products. Developing countries, in turn, have responded by calling for a historical perspective of global deforestation to show that the burden of blame should be shared by all nations engaged in economic development. They contend this would provide a more accurate understanding of the process of deforestation that has occurred over the years—both in developed and developing countries. For most developing countries, forestry is a bread-and-butter issue with forests seen as natural assets that can be used to advance economic development. Forestry revenues help alleviate poverty, which the Food and Agriculture Organization (FAO) identifies as a major cause of deforestation.

The International Tropical Timber Organization (ITTO) became operational in 1986 with the purpose of providing an effective framework for international cooperation between producer and consumer member countries on issues relating to the trade and utilization of tropical timber and the sustainable management of its resource base. Today ITTO continues to assist producer member countries to sustainably manage their tropical forests.

Schisms between environmentalists and those concerned with economic development have narrowed in recent years. Passions ran high in the 1970s and 1980s on both sides of the green divide. In recent years, dissent has been replaced with discussion and some progress has been recorded. According to FAO State of the World's Forests 2001 Report, the net annual forest area loss was estimated to be 9.4 million hectares between 1990–2000, compared to 11.3 million hectares between 1990–95.

All these have some positive ramifications for the world of forestry in the context of sustainable forest management. Forestry is no longer the bogeyman blamed for deforestation. Instead, it is viewed as a responsible way for restoring some of the damage caused by deforestation. Revenues obtained from well-managed natural forests and plantation forests can be ploughed back into developing economies to help raise living standards and arrest forest degradation, which is largely caused by poverty.

WORLD CONSERVATION STRATEGY

Several international organizations have collaborated to develop environmental guidelines for the rest of the world to follow. Foremost among them is the World Conservation Strategy (WCS) published in 1980 by the International Union for Conservation of Nature and Natural Resources (IUCN), United Nations Environment Programme (UNEP) and the Worldwide Fund for Nature (WWF).

WCS sent out a new message: that conservation is not the opposite of development, and it was the first to give currency to the term 'sustainable development'. It emphasized three objectives:
- essential ecological processes and life-support systems must be maintained
- genetic diversity must be preserved
- any use of species or ecosystem must be sustainable.

Since 1980, WCS has been tested by the preparation of national and sub-national conservation strategies in more than 50 countries. It has since contributed significantly to the growing recognition of the need for sustainable development, global interdependence and international equity on matters relating to the environment. In 1987, governments adopted an Environmental Perspective to the Year 2000 and Beyond, which defined a broad framework to guide national action and international cooperation for environmentally sound development. In June 1992, they met at the Earth Summit in Rio to agree on an agenda for the environment and development in the 21st century.

OPPOSITE: Bryophytes such as mosses and liverworts thrive in tropical montane forests 1,500 metres above sea level.

CHAPTER TWO

THE MALAYSIAN RAINFOREST

Malaysia is truly blessed by Mother Nature, and this has never failed to fascinate scientists and adventurers, who have journeyed into its dense, tropical forest in search of its natural wealth and beauty. Malaysia possesses some of the planet's most unique geological formations, coastal features and river systems.

With one of the world's richest and most varied biophysical resources, it ranks as one of 12 'mega-diverse' countries hosting some 185,000 species of fauna and about 12,500 species of flowering plants. All this is densely packed into 330,000 square kilometres of land; 137 kilometres north of the equator, between latitudes 1° and 7° north and longitudes 100° and 119° east; placing Malaysia in the equatorial zone of uniformly high temperatures, high humidity and heavy rainfall—perfect conditions for luxuriant plant growth. Temperatures hover between 24° and 26° centigrade in the lowland forest, with a 0.6° drop for every 100-metre rise in altitude; humidity averages around 80 per cent; and rainfall ranges between 200 and 500 centimetres annually, derived mainly from the monsoons. Generally, there is no pronounced dry season. Not surprisingly, more than half the country is draped in green; from sparse, sandy beach forests to lush lowland rainforests, hill forests and mossy forests on the highlands.

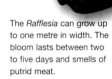

The *Rafflesia* can grow up to one metre in width. The bloom lasts between two to five days and smells of putrid meat.

The country consists of two major landmasses. Peninsular Malaysia, which sticks out like a little finger the size of New York State or England. It occupies 40 per cent of the land mass. Across the South China Sea, on the island of Borneo, lie the states of Sabah and Sarawak, which account for 23 and 37 per cent of the total land area. Together, they are part of the Malay Archipelago, which was formed as a geographical entity about 10–15 million years ago, relatively recent in the history of Planet Earth. While both share an equatorial geographical location, their geological history is markedly different, resulting in a mosaic of landscapes and habitats, from jagged mountain peaks in Sabah and Sarawak to Peninsular Malaysia's languid coast, gently lapped by the sea and studded with offshore islands.

Geologically, Malaysia is composed of four fragments of the earth's crust welded together at different times, in different places. It began as Sundaland 320 million years

OPPOSITE: Rainforest dynamics involve competition to gain a place in the sun.

The moist, damp environment around waterfalls is a microhabitat for mosses and several herbaceous plants such as ferns and begonias.

ago, when it lay below sea level. A spate of magmatic activity about 250 million years ago forced up a wedge of ridges on the earth's crust, creating Malaysia's earliest mountains in central and east Peninsular Malaysia and westernmost Sarawak. Over the years, the mountains were weathered, eroded and submerged and they progressed through a series of successive ice ages and meltdowns. They became a geologically stable part of Malaysia and consisted mainly of sedimentary rock, limestone and peat swamp drained by a few river systems.

The second geological block occurred 240 million years ago with an amputation, when a digit from the grand southern continent of Gondwanaland (origins of modern day Africa, South America, Australia and Antarctica) slipped off, drifting north to attach itself to the peninsula. At the joint, a heave of magma resulted in the igneous rock-based Main Range, the mountain spine of Peninsular Malaysia, rising from bedrock of sedimentary and alluvial deposits.

The third fragment led to the formation of central and north Sarawak and western Sabah, which evolved 90 million years ago when a rift in the South China Sea basin pushed up a crumble of mountains to the surface to form the Crocker Range, the backbone of western Sabah. The last piece of the Malaysian jigsaw is East Sabah, born out of a maverick plate fragment that severed ties with continental Asia, possibly near Hong Kong, and collided into this part of north-east Borneo 19 million years ago. All was well in this entity composed of four fragments until 9–4 million years ago when a granite massif penetrated through a fault line along the folded Crocker Range to rise majestically as the roof of Southeast Asia at 4,095 metres.

The moonscape-like terrain above the tree line of Mount Kinabalu.

OPPOSITE: A few hardy plant species cling to the inhospitable rocky outcrops in Bako National Park, Sarawak.

FOREST COVER IN MALAYSIA

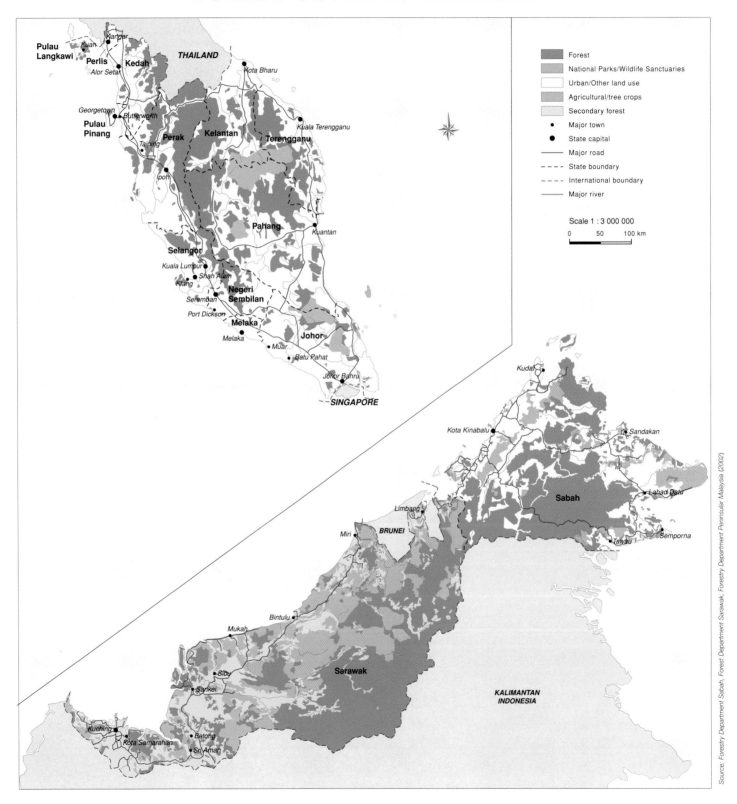

Forest
National Parks/Wildlife Sanctuaries
Urban/Other land use
Agricultural/tree crops
Secondary forest
Major town
State capital
Major road
State boundary
International boundary
Major river

Scale 1 : 3 000 000
0   50   100 km

Source: Forestry Department Sabah, Forest Department Sarawak, Forestry Department Peninsular Malaysia (2002)

FOREST TYPES IN MALAYSIA

1. Mangrove forest
Mangrove forests are known to support only a few hardy plants.

2. Peatswamp forest
Peatswamps are a rich source of timber such as *ramin* and *kempas*.

3. Lowland forest
Found below 300 metres altitude, lowland forests are the most extensive forest type in Malaysia. With a diverse variety of tree species, they are dominated by dipterocarps.

4. Forest on limestone hills
The complex limestone landscape of crevices, caves, cliffs and gullies is home to a large number of plant species.

5. Hill forest
Dominated by dipterocarps, with some species such as *Shorea curtisii* exclusive to them, lower hill forests grow from 300–750 metres and upper hill forests rise to 1200 metres.

6. Montane forest
Dipterocarps are replaced by oaks and laurels in lower montane forests, which occur above the 1,200-metre line.

7. Upper montane forest
Above 1,500 metres, trees become twisted and stunted as seen on Mount Kinabalu.

8. Plantation forest
Commercial timber species such as *Acacia mangium* and *Tectonis grandis* are grown in forest plantations.

Hardy vegetation clinging to a limestone cliff environment.

BOTTOM LEFT: An aerial view of dipterocarp forest in Taman Negara.

BOTTOM RIGHT: Survivors of the harsh environmental conditions on Mount Kinabalu, the highest mountain in Southeast Asia.

Mount Kinabalu is a growing youngster; since its formation, it has grown at the rate of one to two millimetres a year. Geologically, Sabah and Sarawak are still active, with some parts of Sabah growing almost two kilometres over the last two million years. In recent studies, the coasts near Miri and Kota Kinabalu have been seen to display upward growth of a few millimetres a year.

During the course of the 230 million years it took Malaysia's four building blocks to assume their current positions, Planet Earth also underwent alternating phases of global warming and cooling. Sundaland was repeatedly formed and broken up by changes in the sea level. When it dried up, the Malay Archipelago became one vast continent linked by a series of land bridges. Scientists refer to this continent as Malesiana, where flora and fauna were able to extend their range of distribution from the Kra Isthmus in Peninsular Thailand to Papua New Guinea and its adjacent islands in the southeast.

Today, Malaysia's rainforests are amongst the most species-rich type of vegetation in the world. Many species are endemic, found nowhere else in the world. The parade of endemics is the stuff for superlatives: from the mighty dipterocarp tree *keruing jarang* (*Dipterocarpus lamellatus*) to the largest pitcher plant *Nepenthes rajah,* and one of the smallest flowering plants, the orchid *Corybas comptus.* They thrive in the multitude of microhabitats available as a result of recent and past geological history, the warm and moist climate all year round and the infinite variety of soils. These factors also determine the development, distribution and composition of the forests that cloak the country from the coast to the highlands of Kinabalu.

Between the 4,800-kilometre long coastline and Malaysia's highest point at the 4,095-metre Low's Peak on Mount Kinabalu, the broad sweep of Malaysia's landscape passes through many changes of character. Along the coast are sandy beaches with low-density vegetation zones which support hardy staples such as morning glory (*Ipomoea pes-caprae*) that sprawl like flower-speckled rugs on the notoriously nutrient-lacking sandy soil. Their roots dig deep for fresh water, doubling as sand binders checking coastal erosion. Behind them, along the sandy ridges or *permatang* stand the handsome *putat laut* (*Barringtonia asiatica*), *bintangor laut* (*Calophyllum inophyllum*) and *rhu* (*Casuarina equisetifolia*) between dense shrubs and tough grasses such as the *Spinifex littoreus* and screwpine (*Pandanus* spp.) scattered across the sandy coastal landscape. This vegetation reduces soil erosion and fertilizes the sandy soil, with taller trees such as the casuarina acting as windbreaks and providing high-grade firewood. The more inhospitable rocky outcrops, meanwhile, welcome only tufted shrubs and a few species of ferns that burrow around the cliff base, crevices and little islands. The vegetation

The snorkel-like roots of the *api api* (*Avicennia alba*) enable them to adapt to the seaward zone of mangrove swamps.

VEGETATION AND SOIL CHANGES WITH ALTITUDE

NOT TO SCALE

1. **Marine clay**
   Only mangroves can grow in the anaerobic and swampy conditions of marine clay. They have adapted to these conditions by developing 'breathing' roots.

2. **Peat**
   Several commercially valuable timber and palm species grow in acidic peat soils.

3. **Alluvial**
   Plantation agriculture such as rubber and oil palm cultivation is common in the alluvial soils of flood plains.

4. **Lowland hill**
   Healthy dipterocarp forests grow extensively across lowland hill soils that range from iron-rich reddish soils to grey shale-based soils and black volcanic soils.

5. **Limestone**
   Vegetation is sparse and stunted on shallow and peaty limestone soils found on cliffs and pinnacles. On less steep hills, the reddish soils support more lush vegetation.

6. **Upland hill**
   Shorter species of the oak and laurel forest are found on thin upland hill soils.

7. **Montane peat**
   Mosses cling to the peat montane soils on the upper reaches of highlands.

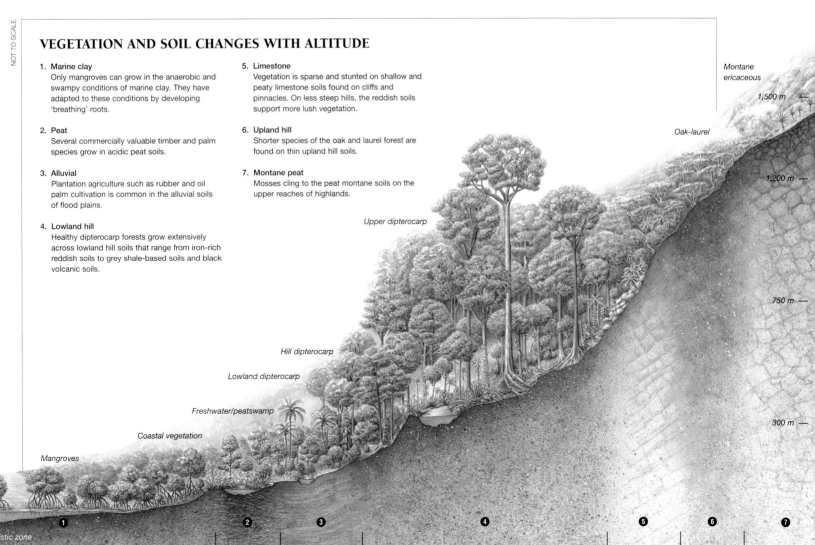

Montane ericaceous

1,500 m

Oak-laurel

1,200 m

Upper dipterocarp

750 m

Hill dipterocarp

300 m

Lowland dipterocarp

Freshwater/peatswamp

Coastal vegetation

Mangroves

Floristic zone

1 2 3 4 5 6 7

The mangrove is home to crustaceans such as the fiddler crab (*Uca* spp.), which can be seen at low tide.

here shares one common feature: the plants are built to withstand water loss through evapotranspiration, either with leaves that are dark green and fleshy, thick and leathery or broad, thin and covered with hair or scales. The fruits and seeds are dispersed by sea currents and are encased in thick and hard or fibrous or spongy coverings that float easily in the water.

The muddy shores of sheltered coasts and river estuaries are fertile ground for the much-maligned mangrove, long dismissed as a blot on the landscape but readily harvested for its fish, prawns and crabs, its wood (*Bruguiera* and *Rhizophora* spp.) and leaves, with *Nypa fruticans* a desired thatch material. Up to a decade ago, there were about 675,000 hectares of mangrove forests in Malaysia, with over half in Sabah, one-third in Sarawak and the rest in Peninsular Malaysia. Mangroves are among the youngest of tropical forests, dominated by a few species that can survive in the harsh swamp environment. Their coastal location means they are slowly but constantly affected by fluctuations in the sea level; vast tracts go under water with sea level increases, only to be reborn during drier periods. In the shorter term on a day-to-day basis, mangrove swamps appear to be threatened by the elements; they are exposed to greater heat, wind, salt spray and solar radiation than other vegetation zones located further inland. The soil here is not favourable either, it is waterlogged, unstable, anaerobic, salty and alkaline.

MATANG MANGROVE MANAGEMENT

The economic value of mangrove forests as fishing grounds is widely acknowledged, with a recent estimate showing that mangrove fish and prawn catches in Peninsular Malaysia were worth well over RM114 million (USD30 million) per year. When managed with restraint and care as demonstrated in the Matang Forest Reserve in Perak on Peninsular Malaysia's west coast, mangrove forests can yield both timber and seafood permanently in what biologists call 'sustained yield exploitation'.

The 40,151-hectare Matang Mangrove, which ranks as the single largest mangrove forest in Malaysia, is often described as the best managed mangrove forest in the world. Some 85 per cent of it is gazetted as productive forest and since 1950

The boardwalk through Matang Forest Reserve, where mangrove ecology can be explored.

harvesting has been carried out on a rotational basis; areas where natural regeneration has not occurred are

restocked through artificial planting. Although it has been a productive forest for nearly a century, it still maintains a complex and fragile ecosystem. To further conserve this forest, the Forestry Department of Peninsular Malaysia has designated a pristine area of 42 hectares of predominantly Rhizophoraceae species forest as Virgin Jungle Reserve.

The forest and mud flats are important feeding and roosting areas for many water birds such as the very rare milky stork (*Mycteria cinerea*) and mammals such as the smooth otter (*Lutra perspicillata*), leopard cat (*Felis bengalensis*), common wild pig (*Sus scrofa*), long-tailed macaque (*Macaca fascicularis*) and the silvered leaf monkey (*Presbytis cristata*).

But mangrove species are master adapters. Some like the *api api* (*Avicennia alba* and *A. marina*) and *perepat* (*Sonneratia alba*), which grow on the seaward zone where the soil is soft, loose and exposed and submerged by low and high tide, have developed ingenious snorkel-style roots that stick out of the soil to obtain their supply of water and oxygen. Further inland in the swamp, which can be divided into zones, each dominated by a single species of tree, vast tracts of *berus* (*Bruguiera cylindrica*) and *bakau kurap* (*Rhizophora mucronata*) thrive. This is the land of stilt-shod mangroves, striking back with their customized weapons—aerial roots, through which water is absorbed osmotically from the substrate in order to survive as a species. In the back mangrove zone of compact, clayey crab mounds grow trees and shrubs such as the *jeruju* (*Acanthus ebracteatus* and *A. ilicifolius*), *kacang kacang* (*Aegiceras corniculatum*) and *api api merah* (*Avicennia intermedia*). Away from the tidal influence, nipa swamp forest and clumps of *nibong* (*Oncosperma tigillarium*) grow on the banks of meandering rivers. The mangrove habitat has practically no undergrowth and never really lacks water, sunlight or essential nutrients. Leaves and fruit continually fall into the water and mud below, providing food for micro-organisms, whose waste products in turn feed fish, prawns and molluscs that live in the shadows of the deceptively quiet and still mangrove swamps.

Freshwater and peatswamp forests attract more life above ground, in the trees where birds nest and feed. They are a veritable birdwatcher's paradise of colourful hornbills, kingfishers, herons and other water birds, which can be spotted or heard when fishing or travelling along the waterways traversing these forests that grow on low-lying river and coastal plains, sometimes in waterlogged conditions below the water level. These productive forests are also home to the proboscis monkey, orang utan, macaques, elephant and water birds. They occupy 2.5 million hectares or eight per cent of the total land area, and are concentrated mainly in eastern Sarawak and in Malaysia's oldest geological zone in Pahang in Peninsular Malaysia. Sarawak alone has more than 1.5 million hectares of these forests on the vast deltas of the Rajang, Baram and Lupar.

CYCLE OF INORGANIC NUTRIENTS IN A RAINFOREST

Rain

Canopy

Uptake

Leaf litter

Throughfall

Forest floor

Rock

Weathering

Roots

Streamflow

Mineral soil

Coastal birds such as the little heron (*Butorides striatus*) are residents of mangrove and freshwater swamps.

WHY FORESTS ARE IMPORTANT: THE CARBON CYCLE

The carbon cycle illustrates how plants and animals of the rainforest rely on each other for survival. Fast growing young trees convert carbon dioxide to organic matter via photosynthesis. In turn, carbon dioxide is released by living organisms into the atmosphere through respiration.

The yellow-vented bulbul (*Pycnonotus goiavier*) is a common resident of urban parks and gardens.

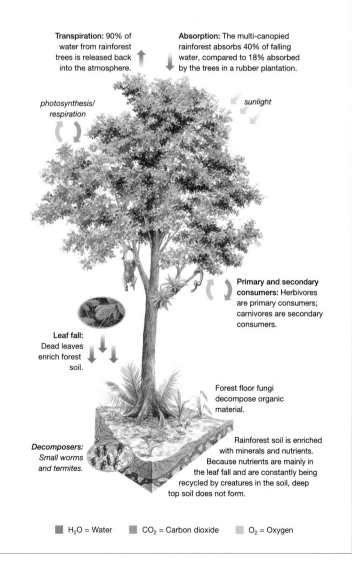

Transpiration: 90% of water from rainforest trees is released back into the atmosphere.

Absorption: The multi-canopied rainforest absorbs 40% of falling water, compared to 18% absorbed by the trees in a rubber plantation.

photosynthesis/ respiration

sunlight

Primary and secondary consumers: Herbivores are primary consumers; carnivores are secondary consumers.

Leaf fall: Dead leaves enrich forest soil.

Forest floor fungi decompose organic material.

Decomposers: Small worms and termites.

Rainforest soil is enriched with minerals and nutrients. Because nutrients are mainly in the leaf fall and are constantly being recycled by creatures in the soil, deep top soil does not form.

■ H₂O = Water   ■ CO₂ = Carbon dioxide   ■ O₂ = Oxygen

NOT TO SCALE

Freshwater swamp forests grow on shallow peat and have fertile subsoil. Peatswamp forests thrive on deep peat, a dark and soupy soil held together by a dense mass of decomposing tree parts. The non-porous soil of these swamps is watered exclusively by rainfall, and they become flooded after a heavy downpour. After prolonged flooding the forest floor dries up. Although they develop at different peat depths, the two share tree species such as *meranti* (*Shorea* spp.), *kempas* (*Koompassia malaccensis*) and *pulai paya* (*Alstonia spathulata*) share a common forest structure: the canopy, understorey and shrub layer. While there is little species variation between the two swamps, there are great variations between different geographical locations. Out of the 289 known peatswamp species, 71 occur in Peninsular Malaysia, 169 in Sarawak and only 49 are common to both localities. The two swamps are logged for their prize timbers, mainly *ramin* (*Gonystylus bancanus*), *kempas*, *meranti* (*Shorea uliginosa* and *S. teysmanniana*), *jongkong* (*Dactylocladus stenostachys*), *sepetir paya* (*Copaifera palustris*) and *kapur paya* (*Dryobalanops rappa*), which account for 70–80 per cent of the large-girth trees (above 60 centimetres) in these forests. Local communities, meanwhile, harvest the edible fruits of shrubs such as *kelubi* (*Eleiodoxa conferta*) and the *pinang raja* (*Cyrtostachys renda*). Screwpine (*Pandanus* spp.) leaves, on the other hand, are used for weavecraft.

Peatswamps are key players in the hydrological and carbon cycles. They are efficient water regulators, acting as a giant sponge, absorbing and storing water in the wet season and releasing it during the dry season. This has prompted the Drainage and Irrigation Department to resort to these natural resources to divert flood waters from rivers such as the Bernam River in Selangor to feeder canals

A crown of *kapur* trees (*Dryobalanops spp.*) at the Forest Research Institute Malaysia (FRIM).

in peatswamps to check flooding of vast paddy lands around Tanjung Karang. On the other end of the scale, peat forests are notorious for their slow burning fires that shroud the surrounding areas with an unhealthy haze. Organic matter does not disintegrate in peatswamps because decomposing agents cannot survive in these oxygen-deprived soils; eventually they break down into hydrocarbons or fossils, the starting point in the formation of fossil fuels such as coal, gas and oil.

From the air, the green cover of Malaysia appears for the most part like a sea of broccoli florets. This is the tree canopy of the dipterocarp forest, *the* celebrated multi-storied moist tropical rainforest, often described as a 'giant green cathedral', that clothes a greater part of the country, from sea level to 1,200 metres. Named after the eponymous tree that dominates the rainforest, dipterocarp forests accounted for 85 per cent of all forested land in Malaysia in 1990. Surveys covering an area of 3,200 hectares in the Jengka Forest Reserve in Pahang revealed that 30 per cent of trees with a diameter of 30 centimetres or more and 55.5 per cent of trees by volume belong to the dipterocarp family.

TASIK BERA WETLANDS

Signed in Ramsar, Iran in 1971, The Convention on Wetlands is an intergovernmental treaty that provides a framework for the conservation of wetlands and their resources. As of July 2002 there were 133 contracting parties to the treaty, with 1179 Ramsar sites, totalling 102.1

A view of Tasik Bera in the state of Pahang.

million hectares. Malaysia nominated Tasik Bera, the largest natural lake in Peninsular Malaysia, as its first Ramsar site in 1995. With a surface area of 38,446 hectares, Tasik Bera is a freshwater habitat and swamp forest, with a high species diversity. The focal point of cultural and agricultural activities of the local Orang Asli (aborigines), the lake is a popular tourist attraction and is also used for scientific research.

The main difference between the lowland and highland dipterocarp forests obviously lies in their plant composition; a large number prefer the warmer lowland temperatures while a few species opt for the cooler highlands, with a few adapting to both environments. While some lowland species are found in the hills, highlanders such as *meranti seraya* (*Shorea curtisii*) are only found in the hills.

Malaysia's lowland and hill dipterocarp forests are amongst the most diverse ecosystems in the world. In Negeri Sembilan at the Pasoh Forest Reserve, a total of 820 species in 294 genera and 78 families of woody plants with a diameter of 10 centimetres or more were recorded in a mere 50-hectare plot. This number represents approximately one-third the total number of tree species found in the Peninsula and exceeds the total tally of woody plant species in the expansive North American continent. Malaysian rainforests are one of the leading world centres for tropical species diversity; it is home to 270 out of the 507 known species of dipterocarp trees; 24 out of 30 known durian species; more than 25 per cent of the world's wild ginger species; 13.4 per cent of orchids and 5.4 per cent of the ferns and fern allies.

Statistics aside, dipterocarp forests also distinguish themselves with their legendary 'roof garden on pillars' structure, not unlike a dense city of skyscrapers, the scene of a competitive environment where everyone races up for a place in the sun. Winning hands down are the kings of the rainforest, the high and mighty dipterocarps that rise up to 60 metres, spreading their crowns over their green domain as the emergent layer in the multi-tiered rainforest. The trunks of most species are dark, fissured and scaly. Other distinguishing marks on their trunks are knobs of resin or *damar*, which help them resist fungal and bacterial infections. Another remarkable feature is their gregarious production habits, which occur irregularly; some species flowering just once every 60 years. When they do, it is with a vengeance: intense flowering and fruiting by nearly all adult dipterocarps trigger off a chain reaction from other trees, transforming the evergreen canopy into a kaleidoscopic whirl of colours.

Occasionally, the dipterocarp's place in the sun is challenged by the *tualang* (*Koompassia excelsa*), a legume that soars even further up to 80 metres. One of the few deciduous trees in the Malaysian rainforest, it is believed to be a relic of the past, when Malaysia's climate was characterized by the four seasons. Honeycombs hang high above in its branches, where the honey producing bee (*apis dorsata*) makes its home.

OPPOSITE: Giant bamboo (*Dendro-calamus giganteus*) soars up to 30 metres at the FRIM grounds in Kepong.

TOP LEFT CLOCKWISE: Forest floor beauty–the herbaceous black lily (*Tacca* sp.)

Forest floor herbs; the species produce varied fruits. *Costus speciosus* is seen here.

Wild ginger (*Zingiber spectabile*).

There are more than a hundred species of *Ficus* in Malaysia including the *Ficus auriculata*.

LEFT TO RIGHT: *Ficus* spp. are known for the elaborate and bizarre root systems.

The woody liana climbs up a host tree seeking sunlight, an essential ingredient for photosynthesis.

The buttresses of the *kasai* (*Pometia* sp.) migrate far across the forest floor.

'Three hundred miles east of Singapore, directly under the equator, lies a vast island clad from centre to circumference with a wonderful and luxuriant growth of unbroken forest.'

WILLIAM T. HORNADAY – 1885

Other forest giants include the *kempas* (*Koompassia malaccensis*) and the latex-bearing *jelutong* (*Dyera costulata*) and *gutta-percha* (*Dichopsis gutta* or *Palaquium oblongifolium*), which are tapped for their sap that is used to make anything from chewing gum to insulation for telegraph wires and for making pipes and golf balls. The emergent layer of tall trees rises like columns from the shallow soils of the rainforest, propped up by huge buttresses. Many of them have rotten trunks, perfect sites for bats, flying squirrels, porcupines and hornbills that live and breed in these hollows.

Below them, the 20–30-metre high main storey and 20-metre high understorey form a continuous forest canopy, effectively blocking most of the sun's rays from reaching the forest floor. Young emergents bide their time here, together with several other trees. The five-metre high shrub level is a generally fairly open area of palms, members of the latex-bearing tree family (Euphorbiaceae) and coffee family (Rubiaceae), and saplings of taller trees. Within this structure lies the mad muddle of the rainforest, where a bewildering array of climbers, crawlers and parasites struggle for space and sunlight in the dense and dark dipterocarp forest. Rattans abseil up tree columns, step by step, using their sharp hooks to climb up their tree ladder; lianas coil around slender tree trunks; epiphytes such as ferns and orchids perch on branches, never to touch the ground; and the bizarre strangling fig (*Ficus callosa*) slowly but surely chokes its host to eventually emerge as a free-standing tree, with a place in the sun.

In Peninsular Malaysia, limestone hills carve a dramatic landscape across the northern states of Perak, Perlis and the 100 plus islands of Pulau Langkawi.

In Sarawak they crop up in Bau, Niah and Gunung Mulu National Park, rising up to 1,700 metres in Gunung Api and Gunung Benarat. Limestone hills are often quarried for stone, especially the Langkawi marble that is sought for its sleek and stylish white sheen and laid on floors of homes and offices. High on the cave ceilings, swiftlets nest, disturbed only by men who risk life and limb to remove their nests, which is essentially swift spittle, for that exotic Chinese delicacy—bird's nest soup. Limestone caverns also house colonies of bats, gregarious creatures that perform one of the most astonishing air shows when thousands of them sweep out of the caves, wheeling and spiralling in the air in their daily flights that take them to their feeding destinations. They feed on small insects and other creatures and in turn are preyed on by hawks perched up on the limestone hills.

The dense forest cover of lowland dipterocarp forest is often given short shrift by limestone pinnacles, jagged summits and other spectacular limestone formations that pierce through the green cover to present what appears to be unprepossessing territory for plant life. Nothing could be further from the truth. The 0.3 per cent of Malaysia's limestone landscape supports 13–14 per cent of Malaysia's known species of flowering plants and ferns! The soils may be abominably poor and shallow, but each limestone hill houses a multitude of microhabitats that are ideal for several species. Balsams (*Impatiens* spp.) and peperomias (*Peperomia* spp.) thrive in the deep shade of the foothills; *Chirita viola* prefer the lightly shaded cliff face; herbaceous paraboeas (*Paraboea paniculata*) grow on arid and exposed cliff faces; and stunted cycads (*Cycas* sp.) are found perched on summits and in crevices, their crooked trunks crowned with large leathery fronds. Less visible is the palm *Maxburretia rupicola*, which burrows itself in the deep crevices of the cliff faces while other limestone dwellers are found in the gullies, cave mouths and underground streams of the limestone hills.

NEXT PAGE: A native tribesman fishing in Tasik Kenyir in the eastern coastal state of Terengganu. A fisherman's paradise, Tasik Kenyir has over 70 varieties of fish.

CANOPY LAYERS OF THE MALAYSIAN RAINFORESTS

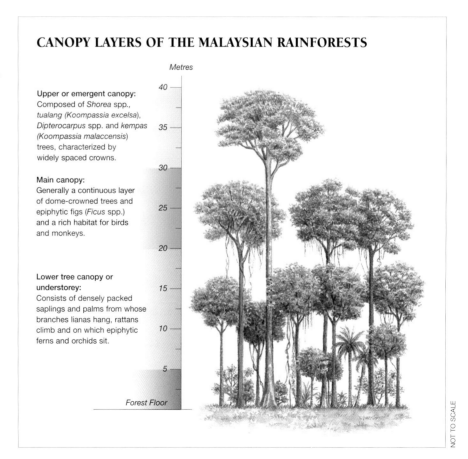

Metres

Upper or emergent canopy:
Composed of *Shorea* spp., tualang (*Koompassia excelsa*), *Dipterocarpus* spp. and kempas (*Koompassia malaccensis*) trees, characterized by widely spaced crowns.

Main canopy:
Generally a continuous layer of dome-crowned trees and epiphytic figs (*Ficus* spp.) and a rich habitat for birds and monkeys.

Lower tree canopy or understorey:
Consists of densely packed saplings and palms from whose branches lianas hang, rattans climb and on which epiphytic ferns and orchids sit.

40

35

30

25

20

15

10

5

Forest Floor

NOT TO SCALE

In Templer Park, to the north of Kuala Lumpur, limestone outcrops such as Bukit Takun emerge starkly above the tree-cloaked terrain.

Moving higher, the dense dipterocarp forest, barring the occasional limestone protrusion, begins to thin out with rising altitude, gradually and subtly until lianas replace large trees. This is montane territory, where the oak (Fagaceae), laurel (Lauraceae) families, myrtle (Myrtaceae) and other temperate staples such as the magnolia, rhododendron, raspberry and an assortment of ferns, orchids, lichens and mosses build one the most picturesque forests in the country. The exact altitude at which montane forests begin to appear varies from 800 metres on small isolated mountains to above 1,200 metres on the slopes of Mount Kinabalu.

There are some marked differences within montane forests themselves, caused in no small measure by falling temperatures. Oak-laurel forest, ferns and orchids of the lower montane forest near the cloud line gradually disappear and there emerges a single layer of trees, dominated mainly by low rhododendrons (Ericaceae) that grow to little over one metre in these cold and damp misty conditions, often clad with lichens, mosses, leafy worts. These are also conducive conditions for attractive pitcher plants and colourful gentians, violets and anemones associated with the colder climes of temperate latitudes.

On the summits and ridges, gnarled trees such as the *gelam gunung* (*Leptospermum flavescens*) and other stunted, spindly, twisted survivors of the cold are wreathed with old man's beard lichen (*Usnea* sp.) and a variety of other epiphytic lichens and

Canopy walkways provide good vantage points to appreciate the rainforest.

RAINFOREST CANOPY WALKS

Suspended tree walkways located high in the tree canopy provide a unique perspective of the rainforest. The canopy walk in Poring Hot Springs, in the northern section of Kinabalu Park, overlooks the rainforest that supports the rare *Rafflesia* and many varieties of orchids exclusive to this part of Malaysia.

The forested grounds of the 1,528-hectare Forest Research Institute Malaysia (FRIM) also has a canopy walk slung 200 metres above the ground. The forest here represents the transformation of a wasteland of abandoned mines, vegetable gardens, shrubby secondary forest and a small plot of virgin jungle into a natural paradise with a waterfall, arboretum and nature trails.

Located in Kepong, 16 kilometres northwest of Kuala Lumpur, it is a popular recreational area. The research centre, which was set up in 1929, is dedicated to promoting sustainable management and optimal utilization of forest resources.

A view of the *kapur* (*Dryobalanops spp.*) canopy. These trees are well-known for their 'crown-shyness', with each crown maintaining its distance from the other.

bryophytes. In Malaysia, windswept shrubby sub-alpine forests occur only on Mount Kinabalu, where the endemic *Leptospermum recurvum* (Myrtaceae) and conifer (*Phyllocladus hypophyllus*) flourish amidst other endemics such as Bornean eyebright (*Euphrasia borneensis*) and Low's buttercup (*Ranunculus lowii*) in grassy, waterlogged mossy conditions. Above the tree line, the cool mountain air shrouds the highland in mist, visibility drops, birdsong ceases and an eerie silence descends in a haunting atmosphere that can only be matched by the harsh heath forests of stunted trees or *kerangas* (meaning 'land where rice will not grow' in the Iban language) that take root on patches of impoverished soils that occur in forested zones across Malaysia.

Given their diversity and luxuriance, natural rainforests are surprisingly bare of flowers and fruits. There are no extravagant splashes of colour from flowering trees; instead, the rainforest is for the most part a heavily textured and layered evergreen locale. Although weather conditions are conducive all year round, many rainforest plants appear to have worked out their flowering-fruiting time slots, with fewer than two per cent of all plants in the dipterocarp forest in this mode at any one time. Given their size and scale, their flowers and fruits are modest, often inconspicuous, in appearance and inconsistent in yield, with good harvests often followed by bad years, resulting in a

Bukit Anak Takun (*Child of Takun Hill*), a smaller limestone outcrop than Bukit Takun in Templer Park.

recurrent cycle of feast and famine for forest herbivores. The majority of dipterocarp forest fruits are tough and unpalatable, with the notable exception of the durian (*Durio* spp.), represented by several species. There are also various wild relatives of the rambutan (*Nephelium lappaceum*), mango (*Mangifera indica*) and breadfruit (*Artocarpus altilis*), some with excellent edible flesh. Then, there are the edible legumes, few in number but diverse in species, that are mainly tall trees, notably the mighty *tualang* (*Koompassia excelsa*) and woody climbers such as the *akar beluru* (*Entada* sp.), whose metre-long pods swing down from the forest canopy.

Mother Nature's handiwork is supplemented by the efforts of Man, who has cleared vast tracts of primary forest to cultivate crops to feed and finance himself. By far the most extensive of man-made habitats in Malaysia are the oil palm and rubber plantations, both introduced species which occupy more than four million hectares on the undulating lowlands. Mature stands offer shade and shelter to many species of insects, birds and mammals such as squirrels, tree shrews and rodents. An increasing number of oil palm estates are installing owl nest boxes to encourage natural breeding of barn owls, which prevent excessive crop damage by pests.

The main food crops include rice, vegetables and tea. Rice is grown in paddy fields in the wetlands, while vegetable gardens and tea estates are located on the dry hill slopes. Green Malaysia also manifests itself in the towns and cities, which are beautifully landscaped with parks, arboreta, botanical gardens and private gardens, where introduced species sit prettily with natives such as the *angsana* (*Pterocarpus indicus*), wild cinnamon trees (*Cinnamomum iners*), palms, brightly coloured shrubs and ground cover, climbers and vines and bamboos. In the *kampung* (village), fruit trees such as the durian (*Durio* spp.), banana (*Musa* spp.), *ciku* (*Manilkara zapota*),

MONTANE FORESTS WATERSHED

Montane forests have an important ecological role. Located high up, near the headwaters of rivers, their canopy breaks the impact of tropical downpours, while the tangled root mass holds the soil together and slows down the downhill rush of water. The waterlogged moss-laden soil, meanwhile, absorbs water, releasing clear water gradually throughout the year. The thick layer of mosses, liverworts and organic debris cladding the tree trunks and branches also soak up water. Removing this protective cover will result in landslides, soil erosion and siltation of waterways, floods and even climatic changes leading to an increase in air temperature.

Mosses carpet the trunks of trees growing in the montane forest in the cool, high altitudes of Gunung Yong Belar near the Perak/Kelantan state border.

ROTTING LOG—A HOME FOR ANIMALS AND PLANTS

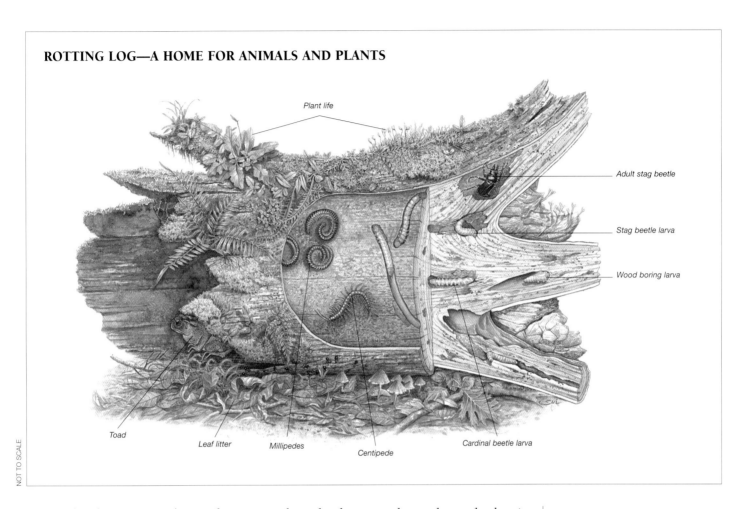

Plant life

Adult stag beetle

Stag beetle larva

Wood boring larva

Toad

Leaf litter

Millipedes

Centipede

Cardinal beetle larva

NOT TO SCALE

guava (*Psidium guajava*), rambutan, medicinal plants such as *hempedu bumi* (*Andrographis paniculata*), *cekur* (*Kaempferia galanga*), *kaduk* (*Piper sarmentosum*) and *serai* (*Cymbopogon* spp.) and ceremonial plants including coconut (*Cocos nucifera*), *kenanga* (*Cananga odorata*), *melati* (*Jasminum sambac*), spices, vegetables and ornamentals are planted. Malaysia's secondary forests may be less complex in structure, but they nonetheless play a vital role in enhancing the environmental, economic and aesthetic value of a country that is well-clad in green.

In the closed and complex rainforest system, the status quo is maintained in a variety of relationships between all life in the forest in a manner mirroring life among men, where collaboration, competition, predation, resistance and specialization are the order of the day. While geared for growth and reproduction for long-term survival, rainforest plants and animals are also geared to fight for their right to survive in their chosen environment, and they do so in a variety of fascinating ways. Plants engage in a variety of moves, partners and strategies in their bid to reproduce. Many of them enlist the help of middlemen such as bats, bees, beetles and birds, attracting them with their

BAT POLLINATION OF THE DURIAN

The *Macroglossus minimus*, a nectarivorous bat, plays a great part in the pollination of the durian (*Durio* spp.), kapok (*Ceiba pentandra*) and *petai* (*Parkia speciosa*) plants. Pushing its head deep into the flower, this cave bat uses its long tongue to sip the nectar. This action results in the bat's head and body becoming dusted with pollen which is dispersed onto the next bloom it visits.

OPPOSITE: The omnivorous slow loris (*Nycticebus coucang*) is one of many dispersing agents that help in forest species propagation.

Found mainly on the forest fringes, the Malay lacewing (*Cethosia hypsea*) butterfly also disperses plant pollen.

bright colour, sweet nectar, fleshy fruit or strong smell in specialized relationships, where the animal acts as the pollinator and is in turn rewarded by the plant with a meal.

Butterflies are drawn to the bright flowers of the *Ixora* spp. and *Mussaenda frondosa* where they sip nectar before flitting off with pollen that gets dusted off on their next *Ixora* feeding ground. The strong odour of aroids (Araceae), *chempaka* (Magnoliaceae) and *sendudok* (*Melastoma malabathricum*) lures beetles that eat the flowers as well as lay their eggs on them. Flies, meanwhile, pollinate the magnificent *Rafflesia* (Rafflesiaceae). These go-betweens help with cross-pollination, which makes plants genetically stronger to adapt to changing conditions such as pests, infection and climate for the long-term survival of the species. Some plants, however, reject third parties and prefer to use their own resources to reproduce and propagate. Many sunflower species (Compositae) are self-pollinators; when their long stigmas do not receive pollen from another of its flowers, they will simply roll back and pick pollen up from the anthers below, enabling the next generation of flowers to bloom.

Seed-scattering animals move over larger ranges than insects, doubling as crowd controllers, helping with the equitable distribution of space in the forest.

The magnificent towering *tualang* (*Koompassia excelsa*) is the tallest tree in Malaysia, reaching heights of up to 80 metres.

Most tropical plants have fruits and seeds specially adapted for dispersal by animals. In Malaysia, there are five groups of dispersing agents: fruit bats, birds, primates, rodents and ground herbivores such as reptiles, fishes and invertebrates. There are at least 15 species of fruit bats that are colour-blind, nocturnal and fly long distances for fruits such as the *ketapang* (*Terminalia catappa*) and *jambu batu* (*Psidium guajava*). Fruit-eating birds such as bulbuls, hornbills and pigeons target the fruits and seeds of the *ara* (*Ficus* spp.) and *kelumpang* (*Sterculia* spp.). The *kera* or long-tailed macaque (*Macaca fascicularis*), white-handed gibbon (*Hylobates lar*), siamang (*Hylobates syndactylus*), orang utan (*Pongo pygmaeus*) and proboscis monkey (*Nasalis larvatus*) forage for *rambutan pacat* (*Xerospermum naronhianum*), *kelat* (*Syzygium* spp.), *pelong* (*Pentaspadon velutinum*) and *sengkuang* (*Dracontomelon dao*). The plants also take precautionary measures to ward off their herbivorous 'partners' from moving in on them too soon and, unwittingly, threatening their survival. To prevent premature eating by these herbivores, unripe fruit is dull-coloured with an unpleasant taste.

Some of the quaintest relationships occur between plants and termites, one of the most common creatures of the Malaysian rainforest. They have evolved a fascinating way of recycling leaf litter, aided and abetted by the fungi, which can do what termites

OPPOSITE: Rugged limestone caves, such as those in Gua Tempurung, Gopeng in Perak, support many microhabitats with several different species of flora and fauna coexisting.

A squirrel feeding on the local fruit *jambu air* (*Syzygium aqueum*).

'Seperti pucuk dengan pelepah.'
Like the shoot and the leaf of the palm.

MALAY PROVERB SUGGESTING MUTUAL
SUPPORT OR A USEFUL ALLIANCE.

THE ANT AND THE EPIPHYTE

The two most common living organisms in the rainforest are ants and plants, who play out their 'I scratch your back, and you scratch mine' role in the grim heath forests of Malaysia. The epiphytic *Myrmecodia tuberosa* houses colonies of ants that build their nests in the swollen protuberances of its stem, which also shields them from their pangolin predators. In the cosy comfort of their plant home, the ants are left to raise their young safely. The ant army, in turn, protects the epiphyte from its marauders, repelling them with their nasty sting. They also feed their host plant with their left-over food and faeces, which are absorbed as nutrition by the epiphyte.

Ant-fern (*Lecanopteris carnosa*) in a tree bough at Genting Highlands.

1. *Myrmecodia tuberosa*
2. *Dischidia major*
3. *Lecanopteris carnosa*

NOT TO SCALE

cannot—produce enzymes that can digest lignin (the basic stuff of wood) and cellulose (the basic stuff of leaves). It begins with termites (Isoptera) eating wood, absorbing the nutrients and excreting lignin, upon which fungi grow. The termites then feed on the fungi and in doing so consume the enzyme that helps them digest leaves. Scientists at Pasoh in Peninsular Malaysia have estimated that nearly one-third of all leaf litter on the forest floor is removed by armies of foraging termites. The next shift of garbage removalists, consisting of bacteria, fungi, earthworms, millipedes, snails and other small creatures then complete the job.

Ants and plants too have a symbiotic relationship, with plants such as the *mahang* tree (*Macaranga triloba*) providing them with food and a home to live and breed in return for protection from foraging herbivores. Ants living in the *Myrmecodia tuberosa*, meanwhile, collect organic and inorganic matter that is absorbed by the root of the plant. The climbing *Dischidia rafflesiana* (Asclepiadaceae) goes beyond the call of duty: it has developed two sets of leaves—normal ones for photosynthesis and larger ant-house leaves that provide shelter to *Crematogaster* spp. and other ants. These leaves are hollow and enlarged with small openings to the chamber near the base of the leaf. The plant's roots grow into the chamber, where they absorb nutrients from the ant's leftover food.

Not all nutrients are used for plant growth; much of it is expended in repelling marauding hordes; especially tiny organisms that have a field day on forest giants, which are helpless in the face of pernicious pest attacks. To fight back, the dipterocarp, for example, has resinous *damar* on its trunk that can gum up the mouth or biochemistry of anything that tucks into it. Their secret weapon, however, is kept well under wraps—cellulose. This hard-to-digest complex chemical lines the walls of each cell in the plant body, making it difficult for animals to get to the nutritious goodies inside, which the trees need for their own survival. Unfortunately, this weapon does not work on big mammals such as the seladang and elephant, which have their own back-up system—millions of microorganisms in their stomachs to break down cellulose. Palms, another popular meal among herbivores, are notoriously physical in their fightback. Rattans, for example, come dressed with long, sharp spines on their stems, leaf stalks and midribs to ward off elephants and hairs on the leaves protect the succulent tissues below that are relished by hordes of insects.

A river flowing through the dense forest at Taman Negara, Malaysia's oldest and most famous national park.

Other plants wage chemical warfare, releasing toxins to stop animals from eating them. The bitter leaves and twigs of the *gambir* (*Uncaria gambir*) and the bark of the *bakau* (*Rhizophora* spp.) contain tannin that wreaks havoc on the digestive system of the diner. Many plants store poisons that are harmless to themselves but convert into lethal doses when released onto the predator. The common *ipoh* or *upas* tree (*Antiaris toxicaria*) contains antiarin, an extremely toxic molecule joined to a sugar, that harms only the enemy. When a herbivore tries to make lunch out of it, the tree produces an enzyme that separates the molecules to release poison into the predator's system. Several other tropical plants including the *Passiflora* spp. and the edible cassava or tapioca (*Manihot esculenta*) resort to using lethal doses of hydrogen cyanide on their predators. The toxin is released in a similar fashion to that of the *ipoh* tree's defences. In the face of the chemical and biological warfare, herbivores such as the proboscis monkey have evolved their own defence mechanisms, mainly in the form of detoxifiers that neutralize the chemical attack. This is just one of many tactics in an evolutionary battle of survival of the fittest that is played out by a cast of many living in this high-density and highly competitive tropical forest stage.

CHAPTER THREE

PLANTS OF THE RAINFOREST

The Malaysian rainforest is like another country, where a seemingly impenetrable fortress of formidable trees defines the border and safeguards the rights and interests of its inhabitants. By sheer size and number, dipterocarps rule this densely populated kingdom of plants and animals. In his book *The Life of Plants*, Professor John Corner FRS, Emeritus Professor of Tropical Botany at Cambridge University, enthuses over them: *'the lofty dipterocarp tree, which represents the culmination of the tropical rainforest in Malaysia, where many species of the family Dipterocarpaceae construct the most luxuriant forest on earth. The immense trunk, superbly engineered..., branches at a height of 100 feet into a large canopy of small leaves, many twigs, and spreading limbs along which animals may travel from tree to tree, and eat, sleep, give birth without returning to the ground. That is the tree of life.'*

Dipterocarp trees are the backbone of the Malaysian rainforest. They rise from the forest floor as 50-metre high skyscrapers in lowland forests and drop down to 20-metre shady columns in the cooler highlands. The exception rather than the rule, taller giants above 60 metres are found scattered in sheltered valleys and foothills of lowland forests. Rainforest trees distinguish themselves as main-storey plants, with thick woody trunks that look like construction piles supported by massive buttresses. Their vertically developed lateral roots prop up the trunk, which in turn holds up the entire forest. The trunk wears a crown of leaves, with mature stands blocking off usurpers from taking their place in the sun. Tree barks are often a clue to their identity; species can be determined by examining their colour, surface type and secretions.

The Dipterocarpaceae family, which includes the genera *Dipterocarpus*, *Hopea* and *Shorea*, grow wild in the multi-layered rainforest that derives its name from its most populous inhabitant. Dipterocarp forests account for 85 per cent of Malaysia's forests, which house at least 270 out of the 507 known species, many of them prized for their timber and by-products. These trees inspire awe by their sheer size and structure; 'Atlas' of the rainforest, their strong and tall frames support other trees and plants in this closed ecosystem. Their daily contribution to rainforest life is mainly confined to

Lichen-encrusted leaf.

OPPOSITE: The massive buttresses of a rainforest tree.

MERANTI TEMBAGA

Fruiting branch of
meranti tembaga

NOT TO SCALE

The light red timber from *meranti tembaga*
(*Shorea leprosula*) is greatly favoured in Europe.

providing arboreal animals with high-rise homes, from which they can move around without ever having to touch the ground. As a source of food, dipterocarps can be unreliable; they participate in mast flowering, synchronized flowering involving several species in the neighbourhood, when sections of the rainforest are ablaze with colours. One tree alone can produce up to four million flowers over a two-week period, with each flower lasting less than a day. They then withdraw from reproductive activities for another few years, when the rainforest returns to its shady hues of green, before another gregarious flowering cycle begins.

The flower sepals enlarge into mature fruits with feathery wings that lend the tree its name: *dipteros* (two wings); *karpus* (fruit). Some species such as the *Shorea* have three wings, while the *Dryobalanops* and *Parashorea* have five wings, frequently red coloured and sometimes green or yellow. Strangely, the wings are more involved in photosynthesis than in seed dispersal, with most seeds falling within 50 metres of tree. As they germinate quickly, dense patches of sprouting seedlings can be seen throughout the rainforest after seed dispersal. Seeds growing close to their parent tend to take advantage of the existing symbiotic mycorrhizal partnerships between certain types of fungus and tree roots. This is where large tree roots ride on fine fungal threads to reach far and wide through the soil to bring water and scarce minerals to feed themselves. Unfortunately, the seeds have low survival rates as they are vulnerable to beetle attacks and are foraged by rodents, even before they fall. The only other family to challenge dipterocarps in terms of number of tall-tree species is the Leguminosae, with its *tualang* tree (*Koompassia excelsa*) recording a maximum height of 80 metres.

In Malaysia about 400 tree species are harvested for timber. The dipterocarp family is the most valuable source of timber with some of the most prized hardwoods in the world. Among the hardwoods obtained from *Shorea* species is *balau* or *selangan batu* (with *batu* meaning 'rock'), an apt description of this heavy hardwood that is sought after for heavy construction, bridges and wharves. As a highly stable wood, it also finds favour in flooring, joinery and even furniture. *Kapur* (*Dryobalanops*), a medium hardwood, is suitable for heavy construction, posts, beams, joists, rafters, flooring and heavy-duty furniture. There are two species of *kapur*—*D. oblongifolia* and *D. aromatica*. The latter, as its scientific name suggests, is a fragrant wood, which is derived from the occurrence of the fragrant oil, Bornean camphor in this medium hardwood. *Keruing* (*Dipterocarpus* spp.) is another medium hardwood. There are 30 species in this timber group, which is utilized for construction. The heavy hardwood of the huge and extensively buttressed non-dipterocarp *merbau* (*Intsia palembanica*) is an attractive timber with a deep colour and a unique interlocked grain. Not surprisingly, it is most highly valued for interior finishing, panelling, strip and parquet flooring, high quality joinery and decorative work. *Kempas*, another non-dipterocarp, is produced by a single species—the *Koompassia malaccensis*, a large, thick tree with high flanges, whose medium hardwood is suitable for parquet, strip flooring and panelling as well as construction work.

I think that I shall never see
A poem as lovely as a tree,
Poems are made by fools like me
But only God can make a tree.

JOYCE KILMER (1886–1918)

Dipterocarp forests contain some of the most prized hardwoods in the world such as *chengal*, *balau*, *kapur*, *merbau*, *meranti*, *kempas* and *keruing*.

The statuesque *Koompassia excelsa* is the source of *tualang*, a medium hardwood with deeply interlocked grains and clearly defined ripple marks. It is easy to work with and is most suitable for construction, heavy duty pallets, flooring and panelling. Another heavy hardwood is the *chengal* (*Neobalanocarpus heimii*) which can be recognized by its dark and fissured bark; its timber is strong and durable and is used in the construction of boats, bridges and the bodies of trucks. Light hardwoods such as the attractive *meranti* (*Shorea* spp.) are popular for interiors. Yellow *meranti*, known locally as yellow *seraya* or *damar hitam* has excellent woodworking properties that make it ideal for panelling, partitioning, furniture, flooring and other joinery applications. Dark red *meranti* (DRM), which is derived from twelve species, has great appeal in Europe, where it is used for exterior joinery. Another highly favoured *meranti* is *meranti tembaga* or copper *meranti* (*Shorea leprosula*). It derives its name from its leaves, whose undersides are covered with rough brownish hair that cast a coppery hue on the tree. This light red timber is used in decorative work, joinery, panelling, shelving, veneer and counter tops.

Durians (*Durio* spp.) are another rainforest staple, with 24 out of 30 known species distributed throughout dipterocarp forests. They are medium to large trees, with sharp buttresses and several have flaky bark. They are one of the best examples of a peculiar rainforest trait—cauliflory and ramiflory flowering and fruiting—a habit they share with the jackfruit (*Artocarpus heterophyllus*). Flowers grow directly on the main stem (cauliflory) and branches (ramiflory) to later become fruits. This disposition may be a strategy adopted by shorter trees to attract different insects to pollinate them, and not vie for the attention of the same pollinating agents as their taller canopy-flowering neighbours. Durian flowers attract bees, beetles, moths and small fruit bats with their copious nectar and accessibility. They develop into large, spiky fruits that split into segments when they are ripe, exposing compartments with fleshy seeds. Durian fruits can not only be seen on the tree trunks; they can also be smelt miles away, especially when they are cracked open to discharge the odorous fleshy parts. Said to be the 'King of Fruits,' some species, however, have small, tasteless fruits.

Most flowering plants are angiosperms that have encased seeds, while many non-flowering plants are gymnosperms ('naked seed' bearers), easily identified by their huge cones. A prominent gymnosperm in the Malaysian rainforest is the conifer, a temperate

OPPOSITE: The attractive pagoda-like crown of the fast-growing *pulai* (*Alstonia* spp.). This non-dipterocarp is a popular choice for urban greening projects.

MERBAU

Merbau leaves

Merbau seed pod

The heavily buttressed *merbau* (*Intsia palembanica*), which belongs to the legume family, produces large, blackish-brown seed pods.

NOT TO SCALE

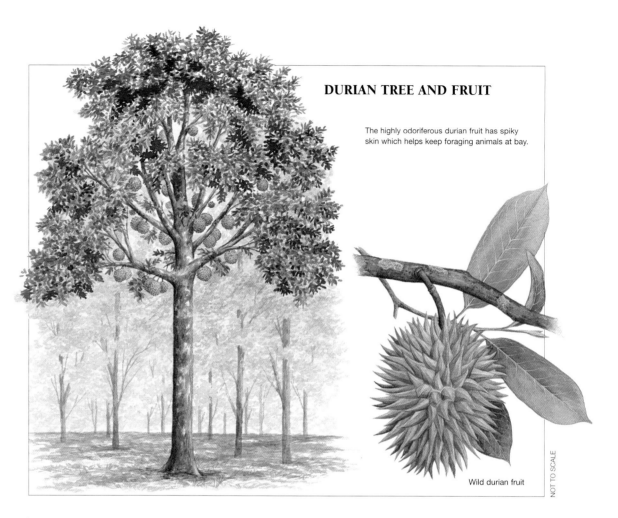

DURIAN TREE AND FRUIT

The highly odoriferous durian fruit has spiky skin which helps keep foraging animals at bay.

Wild durian fruit

NOT TO SCALE

An Orang Asli woman from the Temuan tribe harvesting *damar* (*resin*) from a dipterocarp tree in Sungai Tua, Gombak district, Selangor.

forest staple. Three of the conifer families are native; the rest are introduced species, mainly as ornamentals. The most common native is the *Agathis* genus with six species from the Araucariaceae family. Most of them grow almost to the height of dipterocarps, with which they share a common distinguishing feature: a resinous bark. The mottled, dark grey-brown bark of the *Agathis* flakes off and has a sticky white resin. Dipterocarp bark are sometimes covered with knobs or sheets of *damar*, a viscous fluid that oozes out of the trunk when it is injured. The outer surface hardens into a resinous material, which has many uses. Bees scrape some to seal their home entrances, while villagers burn *damar* to light their homes, to caulk boats and to prepare protective varnishes for timber boats.

Another gymnosperm is the cycad, the wizened old man of the plant kingdom. Conifers and cycads were the most populous flora in the plant kingdom when dinosaurs roamed the planet, with the latter establishing its domination during the 'Age of Cycads' 130 million years ago. Its reign ended 100 million years ago, when cycads were overwhelmed by New World flora, and their numbers were reduced to just three native species of the genus *Cycas* in Malaysia today: *paku laut* (*C. rumphii*), *paku gajah*

(*C. macrocarpa*) and *C. pectinata*. Growing up to seven metres, *C. rumphii* is known locally as *paku laut* (sea fern) because of its location on sandy shores and beach forests. *Paku gajah*, a stouter and darker version of *paku laut*, thrives in lowland dipterocarp forests. Limestone hill inhabitants, *C. pectinata* frequently appears as clumps or jut out of rocky outcrops. Cycads resemble palms with woody trunks crowned by fronds, but the likeness ends there. These forest ancients are sluggish growers, with some species taking as long as two years to mature and germinate the fertilized seed. Highly desirable as ornamentals, their bright orange cones are used in home decoration.

Gnetum, another gymnosperm, is sometimes viewed as the missing link between flowering and non-flowering plants. The plants are cone-bearers but they share angiosperm characteristics in their leaf and cell structure. The missing link theory, however, has been superseded by the studies that attribute the similarities to convergent evolution, where unrelated plants may evolve similar characteristics independently. Most *Gnetum* species in Malaysia are woody climbers, *akar* (lianas) that string themselves across the dark forest. The only free-standing tree is the *belinjau* or *melinjau* (*G. gnemon* var. *gnemon*), widely cultivated for the seeds and leaves, which are used in many food preparations, while the timber is used in house and boat construction.

The *kapur* (*Dryobalanops aromatica*) lives up to its scientific name, emitting a camphor-like odour when the bark is cut.

TOP LEFT CLOCKWISE: The bark of the *jelutong* (*Dyera costulata*) produces copious white latex.

The deeply fissured *tembusu padang* (*Fagraea fragrans*) derives its scientific name from its fragrant white flowers.

Bark of the *sepetir daun nipis* (*Sindora echinocalyx*), a light hardwood species.

Keruing bulu (*Dipterocarpus baudii*) has light-coloured scaly bark and hairy leaves.

The cankered bark of the *mempisang batu* (*Monocarpia marginalis*).

Meranti pa'ang (*Shorea bracteolata*) has dark grey-brown bark with irregular fissures.

WATER WORLD—MALAYSIA'S AQUATIC PLANTS

Malaysia has about 216 aquatic plants that occur in freshwater bodies such as ponds, lakes, dams, rivers and wet paddy fields. Most of them are considered weeds; they are prolific, regenerating sexually or asexually and are tolerant to a wide range of environmental conditions. The dense growth of duckweed (*Lemna perpusilla*), for example, obstructs sunlight from penetrating the water, causing the oxygen level to drop and literally chokes marine life to death.

Aquatic plants fall into three groups: free-floating plants, submerged plants and emergent plants. Free-floating aquatic plants generally have flowers and leaves exposed at or above the water.

Sea grasses are submerged plants, which grow in shallow, coastal waters, where they act as stabilizers and provide shelter to marine life species that use them as feeding and breeding grounds.

The *telipok* or water lily (*Nymphaea lotus*), which was introduced from Egypt, is propagated from rhizomes.

Emergent species are rooted in the muddy substrates of shallow water bodies, where their stems are partially above water.

There is yet another group of plants referred to as amphibious plants that can grow both in water (submerged) and out of water (emerged). Intrepid survivors, they adapt remarkably well to either terrestrial or underwater conditions when necessary.

More than 15 species of aquatic plants are edible. The lotus ranks as the most popular; all parts of it can be eaten, from fruit to seed and rhizome. Other local favourites are the *genjir* (*Limnocharis flava*), Chinese water chestnut (*Eleocharis dulcis*) and *kangkong* (*Ipomoea aquatica*).

Species belonging to the grass and sedge families are harvested and used as animal fodder and fertilizer. *Jerangau* (*Acorus calamus*), *chengkeru* (*Enhydra fluctuans*) and *jeruju* (*Acanthus ebracteatus*) are used for medicinal purposes. Species such as *Blyxa echinosperma* and *Ceratophyllum demersum* generate oxygen and ornament fish aquariums. The leaves and stems of *Lepironia articulata* and *Pandanus helicopus* are used to make handicrafts.

The forest under-storey is a botanical paradise of evergreen flowering shrubs, ranging in height from 50 centimetres to five metres. The *simpoh ayer* (*Dillenia suffruticosa*) has large, broad leaves and is a shade-tolerant plant that thrives in moist lowland and swamp forests; others such as the rhododendron family and conifers of the *Dacrydium* spp. have short, linear leaves and their preferred habitat is the montane forest. Most of them are ornamentals, with dazzling flowers. The *sendudok* (*Melastoma malabathricum*) has large pink flowers; the introduced *Calliandra emarginata* has fluffy flowers characteristic of mimosas (Mimosaceae); while another non-native, the pristine white *Gardenia jasminoides* (Rubiaceae) flowers exude a heavenly scent.

The most significant shrub in Malaysia must surely be the *Hibiscus*, whose *H. rosa-sinensis* has been adopted as the national flower. There are several *Hibiscus* species, usually profuse with blooms, ranging from pure white to brilliant red and yellow. Some such as the national flower are elegant single-layered five-petal flowers; others are more robust multi-layered varieties. The blooms do not last for more than a day, but flowering is profuse. Another common shrub is the *Ixora javanica*, with its clusters of starry red, orange and white flowers. Like the *Hibiscus*, it is rarely devoid of flowers and is a cheerful plant of the rainforest, homes and parks.

It is hard to believe the fabulous-looking ferns could have anything in common with the fungi, algae and bryophtes. But they do. They are all non-

The *Hibiscus rosa-sinensis* was proclaimed the national flower of Malaysia on 28 July 1960. This shrub flourishes all over Malaysia. The bright red colour of the flower is interpreted as a symbol of bravery.

flowering plants that have no fruits or seeds and share a common method of propagation: tiny spores. Malaysia's moist rainforests are a hot favourite with ferns and fern allies, with more than 650 species, approximately 5.4 per cent of the world total, growing in wild abandon in lowland and, more so, in highland forests such as Gunung Tahan, Mount Ophir, Cameron Highlands, Fraser's Hill and the Endau-Rompin Reserve in Peninsular Malaysia. Collectively known as pteridophytes, they vary in size from the magnificent tree fern (*Cyathea contaminans*), with its four-metre long leaves and high slender trunk to that modest fern ally, the club moss (*Lycopodiella cernua*), whose 1.5-millimetre leaves can easily escape the naked eye. But the club moss has the last word; it has the distinction of being among the first in the plant kingdom to have developed passages within their tissues to transport food and water for its survival.

They display a great variety in their leaf structures; some are water-sensitive, others as tough as they can come. Upright ferns such as the elephant fern (*Angiopteris evecta*) have firm and fleshy leaves that wilt with water loss. Filmy ferns belonging to the Hymenophyllaceae family prefer to creep along the rocky forest floor and along streams, spreading out their finely dissected leaves to absorb moisture from the air. Moisture deprivation causes withdrawal symptoms, and the leaves curl up until they are replenished once more.

A praying mantis is attracted to one of the many colourful flowering plant species that grow in Malaysia.

Flamboyant ferns (*Cyathea* spp.) with four-metre lacy leaves.

NEXT PAGE: The rainforest is home to some native tribes in Malaysia.

 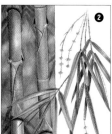   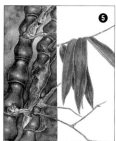 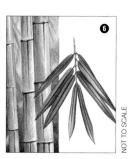

NOT TO SCALE

Malaysia has 80 species of native and introduced species of bamboo, which belong to the grass family.

1. *Gigantochloa scortechinii*
2. *Schizostachyum gracile*
3. *Maclurochloa montana*
4. *Schizostachyum brachycladum*
5. *Bambusa vulgaris* cv. *wamin*
6. *Bambusa vulgaris*

Climbers are somewhat tougher, and climbing ferns *Teratophyllum* and *Lomariopsis* begin life as creepers, spreading across the forest floor until they find a tree to latch on to begin their upward surge, their root-stems hooking onto the bark of the host. Even hardier are thicket-forming ferns such as the *resam* (*Dicranopteris linearis*) and bracken (*Pteridium aquilinum*), which grow in harsh, sun-baked land. Once they take root, they are hard to displace. Even fires cannot destroy bracken, whose underground stems ensure their long-term survival. Their steadfast attachment to the soil makes them highly efficient ground cover, retarding soil erosion.

Epiphytic ferns are even more stunning than their terrestrial cousins. Riding high on the branches and canopies of forest trees, spectacular ferns such as the oak leaf fern (*Drynaria quercifolia*), stag's horn fern (*Platycerium coronarium*) and bird's nest fern (*Asplenium nidus*) tend to overshadow their hosts. More than half of Malaysia's ferns are epiphytes, growing off the ground and on someone else's turf. But they are no parasites. They are found sitting high up, looking proud that they can fend for themselves with their water-retentive and multi-functional leaves, the latter usually serving as feeding and reproductive mechanisms. The oak leaf fern, for example, has two sets of leaves: nest and foliage leaves. The former are the food store, collecting nutrient-charged rainwater, debris and humus to feed the roots; the latter (longer shredded leaves) are the reproduction zone. The stag's horn fern, meanwhile, has three types of leaves—green upright leaves for photosynthesis, basket leaves for food collection and pendulous dissected leaves for propagation. Nest and

THE BAMBOO CURTAIN

Bamboo is the common name for approximately 480 species of perennial, woody, shrubby or tree-like plants. In Malaysia, there are 80 species of both native and introduced bamboo that range from 30-metre-high skyscrapers to diminutive 30-centimetre plants. Although bamboos are widespread in the tropics and subtropics, species such as *Bambusa vulgaris* and other native species have restricted distribution. For example, the *B. farinacea* and *Gigantochloa scortechinii* are endemic to Malaysia.

Most of them are erect and tend to grow profusely, producing impenetrable thickets in some areas. They can also be rapidly invasive, overtaking forest sites and open areas, retarding the recovery of the original forest.

Flowering habits of bamboo species vary from flowering irregularly and plants staying alive afterwards to mast flowering involving most or all the clumps in a large area. Species such as *G. scortechinii* and *Schizostachyum zollingeri* display this flowering habit, when all members of the species flower at the same time and die shortly after that. Regeneration from the remaining rhizomes may occur. In some species there is also continuous flowering without immediate mortality. Some species may even exhibit different flowering behaviour from their typical behaviour in extreme weather conditions, such as a drought.

Bamboo trunks are used for water pipes, boat masts and in construction.

EPIPHYTIC FERNS ON A RAINTREE

1. Stag's horn fern (*Platycerium coronarium*)
2. Bird's nest fern (*Asplenium nidus*)

NOT TO SCALE

basket leaves may serve as homes for other epiphytes, ants and small animals. The fern nests also have the bonus of being a food pantry. Clusters of fern rhizomes found locked around host branches are cosy homes for some small life forms such as the ants that live and feed in hollow rhizomes of the ant-fern (*Lecanopteris carnosa*), which in turn absorbs their leftovers and excreta in a mutually beneficial relationship.

Another plant whose beauty lies in its leaf is the palm, with some fan palms the toast of the plant kingdom for having the most unusual leaf structure. Malaysia has more than 80 species of fan palms, which include the *Licuala cordata*, *L. longicalycata*, *Johannesteijsmannia magnifica* and *Livistona endauensis*. *Licuala* spp. are exquisitely photogenic palms of the forest undergrowth, with unmistakable wedge-shaped leaflets. More diverse are feathered palms that belong to the *Pinanga, Areca* and *Iguanura* genera. The fishtail (*Caryota mitis*) has jagged-margin leaflets and double pinnate leaves while the *Arenga undulatifolia* is conspicuous with its large green leaflets with striking wavy

The stag's horn fern has a humus nest that traps falling organic matter for the plant to feed on.

OPPOSITE: Lianas are a mainstay of all tropical rainforests; these woody climbers twist around and loop across other plants in their upward ascent for sunlight.

margins. Other *Arenga*, the *distincta* and *borneensis*, are short undergrowth palms with slender reed-like stems and small fishtailed leaflets. *Pinanga veitchii* attracts attention with its striking colours and darkly mottled, pale-maroon coloured young leaves that have a purplish undersurface. Many palms are viewed as ornamentals, and rate highly among proud homeowners and urban landscape architects.

Palm flora is a major flower and fruit bearing community in the rainforest. The Calamoideae consisting of rattans (*Calamus* spp.), *salak* (*Salacca glabrescens*) and wild sago (*Eugeissona utilis*) have scaly fruits and spiny leaves. Other groups such as the coconut (*Cocos nucifera*) and *areca* nut (*Areca catechu*) are encased in husk. While palms can be identified by their flowers and fruits, they are best recognized by their leaves. Generally, there are several hardy species, growing wild in a variety of habitats from swamps to limestone hills and montane forests. Soil types are believed to determine their distribution. Palm flora is most diverse in the rainforest, where they dominate the understorey up to 1000 metres above sea level. Here

PALM HABITATS AND ECOLOGY

There are over 510 species of palms (indigenous and introduced species) found throughout Malaysia. Some species require specific habitats, while others are tolerant of a variety of habitats.

Lowland and hill forests
6. *Iguanura wallichiana* is a small palm common in the lowland rainforest undergrowth.

7. *Arenga westerhoutii*, an arborescent palm, is a distinctive element of the lowland rainforest canopy.

8. The genus *Licuala* is frequently found dominating the forest floor, but many species have a very restricted distribution.

9. *Plectocomia elongata*, a flexible climbing palm, reaches beyond the canopy with the help of backward-pointing spines.

Montane forest
10. *Pinanga perakensis* is an endemic feather-leafed palm found only in montane forest.

Peatswamp forest
4. *Cyrtostachys renda* is the dominant palm of the undisturbed peatswamp forests of Perak, Selangor, Johor and Sarawak.

Mangrove swamp
1. & 2. A colony of *Nypa fruticans* and *Phoenix paludosa*. Communities of *P. paludosa* are sometimes found in the brackish inland margins of the mangrove forest, otherwise dominated by *N. fruticans*.

3. *Oncosperma tigillarium* commonly occurs on the landward side of coastal areas.

Limestone hill
5. *Maxburretia rupicola*, a palm species that inhabits limestone hills. It is confined to Bukit Takun and the Batu Caves in Selangor.

1,500 m

1,200 m

750 m

300 m

NOT TO SCALE

STRANGLING FIG DEVELOPMENT

1. Fig seeds are dispersed by animals onto the host tree branches where they grow into epiphytic bushes.

2. From there, roots quickly begin to spread down the trunk of the supporting tree to the ground.

3. Side roots encircle the trunk. The branches begin to spread through the crown of its support.

4. After a long struggle, the host tree eventually dies and the fig tree finally stands on its own.

NOT TO SCALE

is found most of Malaysia's impressive collection of indigenous palm flora: close to 400 species in 33 genera. Some are tall freestanding trees such as the massive tree palm, *bayas* (*Oncosperma horridum*), the giant fishtail palm (*Caryota maxima*) and an assortment of *Arenga, Borassodendron, Eugeissona, Livistona, Oncosperma, Orania* and *Pholidocarpus*. Closer to the ground are the short, stemless palms such as *Iguanura wallichiana* and climbers such as rattan.

With most rattans, it is a case of 'look but don't touch'. They are some of the thorniest plants in the rainforest, with enough sharpness to seriously injure hapless animals and intrepid adventurers and naturalists such as William T. Hornaday. In his *Two Years in the Jungle: The Experiences of a Hunter and Naturalist in India, Ceylon, the Malay Peninsula*, first published in 1885, he wrote: '*Magnificent spreading palms* (Livistonia sinensis) *grew thickly everywhere; beautiful to the eye their long, slender stems were, but always set with rows of stout and sharp thorns, curved just the wrong way for comfort, and always ready to catch a passing victim. The branches of the worthless climbing rattan* (Calamus) *were particularly cruel. This species is very abundant, climbing over the underbrush and sending out many slender branches which droop like those of the weeping willow. The end of each is leafless for about two feet from the tip, and the slender, supple stem resolves itself into a row of animated trout-hooks. The way those threadlike stems will reach out to seize a victim and then hang on, is enough to believe them the invention of the devil. One will catch you suddenly...and rakes you across the cheek like a fine saw, cutting a neat little gash as it goes.*

Orang Asli collect the long and supple vines of the rattan, which are ideal for making furniture.

Again, one will spring and lay hold of your neck with a score of needlelike points, while others fasten themselves in your clothes, or upon your bare hands.'

Ageing rattans, however, lose their bite. The thorns on the leaves and leaf sheaths eventually rot and die to expose smooth canes underneath. These long, supple and pliable vines are harvested for domestic and commercial use—for furniture, weaving, twine, food and medicine. Rattans are found exclusively in tropical and subtropical forests, mainly as climbers that can grow to great lengths; the longest recorded was more than 175 metres. Rattans grow in profusion in Malaysia, which is home to 200 species out of the world total of 600.

Rattans appear to collaborate with woody climbers to form tangled curtains of vines in the rainforest, by twisting around and looping across the trees in their upward ascent for light. From stringy, herbaceous creepers to tough woody perennials, these aggressive plants have only one aim: to race up from any vacant spot in the ground for the strong and healthy dose of sunshine essential for their survival. Climbers are most rampant in secondary forests and at the edges of forest where breaks in the vegetation are more readily available.

Since they do not have to support their own weight, climbers tend to expend all their energy on their rapid rise, sometimes growing from two to five metres a year and reaching more than one kilometre in length. Fortunately, they are blessed with efficient 'plumbing' systems to pump up moisture and nutrients from their roots to their foliage. Climbing mechanisms, however, vary between species. Some such as *Aristolochia* spp. and *Fibraurea* spp. and *akar* (lianas) are twiners; *Artabotrys* spp. and *Uncaria* spp. use hooks; the *Gloriosa superba, Clematis triloba* and *Bauhinia* spp. twirl around their supports with their tendrils; pandans (*Pandanus* spp.), figs (*Ficus* spp.), aroids (Araceae) and pepper (*Piper nigrum*) use their roots; while rattans are notorious for their thorns.

The latticed roots of a strangling fig (*Ficus* sp.) that eventually choke the life out of the host tree.

EIGHT GINGER SPECIES

Bunga kantan (*Etlingera elatior*) is an essential ingredient in Malay dishes such as *laksa* and *asam pedas*.

The handsome inflorescence of *tepus tanah* (*Zingiber spectabile*) is much sought-after for floral arrangements.

1. *Hedychium longicornutum*
2. *Alpinia javanica*
3. *Zingiber spectabile*
4. *Etlingera corneri*
5. *Globba patens*
6. *Amomum uliginosum*
7. *Elettariopsis triloba*
8. *Scaphochlamys concinna*

NOT TO SCALE

AN EXTREMELY VERSATILE FRUIT—THE BANANA

One plant that is found in most Malaysian backyards is the *pisang or* banana (*Musa* spp.) tree. There are over 40 varieties of banana in Malaysia, which is one of the leading producers of banana in the world. Some bananas grow wild in the jungle; some are garden varieties, while a few such as the hardy *berangan* and *awak* have graduated to become orchard species. The banana is also one of those versatile plants (another is the coconut) that can be used from crown to root. The plant starts flowering between seven to twelve months old, and the fruits are ready for harvesting in eight weeks. The trees bear fruit only once, which has inspired the Malay proverb, '*Pisang tidak akan berbuah dua kali,*' (the banana does not fruit twice), the equivalent of 'Opportunity only knocks once'.

The fruit that is the most prized item, can be eaten raw or cooked, which in turn has led to a dazzling array of banana-based recipes. Most common is *pisang goreng* (banana fritters), a popular local snack. Another banana dish is *pengat pisang*, a coconut milk, sago pearls and sugar delicacy, which is a tasty dessert.

Varieties favoured for cooking are *pisang nangka, pisang tanduk* and *pisang*

The black-naped oriole (*Oriolus chinensis*) feeding on one of the many varieties of bananas (*Musa* sp.).

awak while *pisang rastali*, *pisang berangan*, *pisang mas* and *pisang embun* are best when eaten raw.

Banana leaves play a vital part in retaining the flavours of the food. The very Malaysian *nasi lemak* (rice steamed in coconut milk) is almost always wrapped in banana leaves and South Indian restaurants serve food on banana leaves, which are disposed of after the meal.

The banana plant is closely connected with the Hindu religion, and a banana tree is cut and put up at the entrance of the home and temples at weddings as a symbol of fertility and prosperity. Banana sheafs are must-haves in temple ceremonies.

The plant also has a dark side to it. According to local lore, the banana tree is the abode of the beautiful female ghost known as *Pontianak* who lives in the heart of the tree.

Bananas are also used in traditional medicine. Chinese traditional medicine classifies the banana as a *yin* ingredient, which can be used to establish the 'yin-yang' balance in the body. It is used to help lower high blood pressure. The flowers are used to treat bronchitis and dysentery, while cooked banana flowers are recommended for diabetes. The young leaves are used as poultices on burns and other skin afflictions while the root is used to treat digestive disorders.

Big woody climbers are the most prevalent in the Malaysian forest, climbing successively taller trees, sometimes extending across as many as 27 tree crowns. Unchecked, the weight of thick woody climbers (*Milletia* spp.), can cause walls of trees to collapse. Some hosts find themselves deprived of their share of sunlight and will eventually die. Climbers, which account for eight per cent of Malaysia's flowering flora, add splashes of colour to the predominantly green jungle canopy. The rest of the forest, is livened up with flowering herbs, which constitute 30 per cent of flowering species in the country. There are eight major flowering herb families in Peninsular Malaysia: the grasses (Graminae), sedges (Cyperaceae), coffee family (Rubiaceae), African violets (Gesneriaceae), acanthus family (Acanthaceae), aroids (Araceae), orchids (Orchidaceae) and the ginger family (Zingiberaceae). Each group has more than a hundred species. It is a slightly different head count in Sabah and Sarawak, which show a predisposition for fewer Acanthaceae species and more begonias (Begoniaceae) and orchids.

NEXT PAGE: Masterful mangrove adaptation—the stilt roots of the *Rhizophora* help anchor the trees on unstable, muddy terrain.

A drop in temperature triggers the mass flowering of the pigeon orchid (*Dendrobium crumenatum*).

Generally, herbs are non-woody, soft-leafed flowering plants, with just one embryonic seed leaf. They range from the minute moss-like *Malaccotristicha malayana* to the massive *keladi* (*Alocasia robusta*) and wild bananas that grow up to nine metres. Some are short-lived annuals such as *Hedyotis dichotoma*, a relative of the coffee family (Rubiaceae), which completes its life cycle within three months; others are slow-growing perennials such as *Didymocarpus platypus* that takes about three months to produce a new leaf and lives more than 20 years. Several perennials have gained a reputation as the immortals of the forest floor; even their leaves have long lives, recording a life span of 18–33 months compared to six to 12 months for the leaves of big trees. Most are attractive, bearing lovely flowers. Species-rich herbs such as *ati-ati gajah* (*Sonerila*) bear dainty flowers; *Didymocarpus* has trumpet-like flowers; and *Argostemma* has delicate star-shaped blooms.

The most flamboyant herb growing in the gloom of the forest floor is the ginger, with its blooms in hues of brilliant red and orange, crawling or standing erect in the lowlands between 200–500 metres above sea level. They have modified underground stems, which tend to run across the forest floor, only to stop at regular intervals to send up vertical leaf-bearing stems. Among the most spectacular of ginger flowers is the red cone-like inflorescence of *tepus tanah* or earth ginger (*Zingiber spectabile*) which grows up to two metres high. Other ginger beauties are clumps of *Alpinia* and *Etlingera* species that grow up to more than three metres high and have showy heads of inflorescence. Some ginger flowers are tiny, including the rosette-like flowers of the peacock ginger (*Kaempferia pulchra*) and the smallish *Camptandra parvula*, that grows to no more than five to ten centimetres high.

Hedychium longicornutum is among the few epiphytic gingers thriving in the Malaysian tropical forest. The hardy *Alpinia ligulata*, *A. mutica* and a few species of *Zingiber* thrive in the swamps, while *Boesenbergia curtisii* and *K. pulchra* are endemic to limestone habitats. Many of these species have been cultivated as ornamentals for public

Orchids are the basis of a thriving cut flower industry in Malaysia.

and private gardens. But cultivated ginger represents only about six per cent of the 177 species found in the Peninsula and 173 species found in Sabah and Sarawak, which belong to the Indo-Malayan region, the centre of diversity for the ginger family.

Crushed ginger leaves emit the familiar ginger fragrance; but as food and medicine, it is the root that counts. The sharp and piquant taste of *halia* (*Zingiber officinale*) makes its presence felt in several Malaysian ethnic cuisines. *Lengkuas* (*Alpinia galanga*) and the inflorescence of *bunga kantan* (*Etlingera elatior*) are basic ingredients in Malay dishes such as *rendang* and *laksa* respectively. About seven to eight per cent of ginger species have medicinal properties, with *lempoyang* (*Zingiber zerumbet*), *cekur* (*Kaempferia galanga*) and *lengkuas ranting* (*Alpinia conchigera*) used widely to treat swellings and bacterial infections. Ginger and turmeric (*Curcuma domestica*) are also commonly used in *jamu* concoctions, traditional herbal health and beauty products.

Without a doubt, the orchid is one of the most exotic and celebrated rainforest plants. The Orchidaceae family has the largest contingent of flowering plants in the plant kingdom and its floral structure ranks the orchid as the most advanced and distinctive flowering plant. Orchid sepals and petals tend to look alike, except for one petal that droops like a lower lip. With most of them, the pollen-bearing male stamen is fused with the female stigma and style to form a column. This restricts insects from slipping from the stamen to stigma of the same flower, thus ensuring cross-pollination. Most orchids also need a reasonable amount of sunlight. A majority of Malaysian orchids are thus epiphytes, sporting swollen stems bases to store water, as they perch on branches, tree trunks, and even rocks, reaching out for their quota of sunlight.

Of the world's 25,000 orchid species, more than 850 occur in Peninsular Malaysia and are commonly found in Gunung Jerai, Cameron Highlands, Genting Highlands, Gunung Ledang and Penang Hill. Another 2,500 are

This *Piper* sp. is an attractive forest floor plant that belongs to the pepper family of creepers and climbers.

RAFFLESIA BLOOMING PHASES

a. *Rafflesia* buds develop from minute strands spread through the host's stem tissues.
b. The *Rafflesia* bud breaks through the host's bark.
c. Nine months later, the mature bud is the size of a small cabbage.
d. The putrid-smelling open bloom lasts only from two to five days.

NOT TO SCALE

found in Sabah and Sarawak. With 1,200 species, the concentration of wild orchids on Mount Kinabalu surpasses that found anywhere else in the world! The largest is the showy tiger orchid (*Grammatophyllum speciosum*), with its two- to three-metre long inflorescence of speckled large flowers. The *Phalaenopsis violacea* has attractive sprays of five-centimetre flowers in varying colours of white to deep purple. Easily overlooked, however, is the *Corybas* spp., one of the smallest orchids in the world growing no more than a few centimetres high. There are also distinct variations between their leaves: a Sabah endemic, the elephant ear orchid (*Phalaenopsis gigantea*) lives up to its name with its huge, droopy, succulent leaves, 60 centimetres long and 20 centimetres wide. The *Taeniophyllum obtusum*, on the far end of the scale, is devoid of all leaves. Jewel orchids have ornate leaves, the *Calanthe pulchra* has pleated palm-style leaves, and the *Dendrobium* species have run-of-the-mill narrow, leathery leaves. Then there are the fragrant blooms of *Vanda deari* and *Vanilla pilifera* that exist in an exalted world compared to the *Bulbophyllum maximum*, an attractive but rather pungent smelling bloom.

There is great world demand for orchids, which are grown as ornamentals and sought as cut flowers. While some blooms last only a day, some varieties, especially the *Phalaenopsis* species, can last for weeks. The rare *P. violacea* and *Paphiopedilum rothschildianum* are collectors' items, with a hefty price tag over their heads. Herein lies the threat to orchids, with economic benefits outweighing ecological considerations. To protect rare and endangered species, several orchid conservation and research centres have been established since the 1980s in several parts of Sabah and Sarawak.

Evolution is not always for the better. For some plants, it means that they have to lose their independence and become parasites living off the goodness of others. However, many parasites do not appear to suffer from an image problem; instead, some such as the *Rafflesia* are heaped with accolades for rewarding the Malaysian rainforest with the world's largest flower, with some species of *Rafflesia* flowers weighing up to seven kilograms and measuring one metre in diameter. As a holoparasite, the *Rafflesia* have no leaves, no chlorophyll and no roots; instead they pierce the host's stem with fine masses of haustoria growing on thread-like stems. Once attached, the haustoria tap on the host to feed the rest of the plant.

The *Rafflesia* feeds off some species of *Tetrastigma* (Vitaceae), a woody climbing vine, to produce a single, putrid but magnificent bloom. *Christisonia* and *Aeginetia* from the Scrophulariaceae, which parasitize bamboo roots, also produce large showy flowers. The tuber-like vegetative body of another holoparasite, the *Balanophora*, which lives off the roots of montane trees, produces inflorescences of tiny flowers, with some as small as one millimetre in size. The seed size of *Rafflesia* is uniformly small.

Hemiparasites appear to have moved up the evolutionary cycle; they have green leaves for photosynthesis but rely on their host for water and nutrients. Some such as the scurfy mistletoe (*Scurrula ferruginea*), live on trees including fruit trees and are unwelcome intruders. If the mistletoe is not removed it causes irreparable damage to the host tree and will quickly spread to other trees, which could be disastrous in an orchard. Classified as a weed, the mistletoe's seed dispersal strategy is guaranteed to succeed, ensuring its survival. Dispersed by birds, mistletoe seeds contain a sticky inner layer that pass through the bird's gut, eventually being disposed of in the normal fashion. Now the sticky seeds are attached to the bird's anus. When the bird alights on the host to get its fill of mistletoe seeds, it rubs its anus on the branches to be rid of the sticky seeds, causing mistletoe seeds to fall directly onto the host branch.

THE EIGHT *RAFFLESIA* SPECIES FOUND IN MALAYSIA

1. R. arnoldii ø 90–107cm
2. R. kerrii ø 100cm
3. R. hasseltii ø 45–50cm
4. R. tengku-adlinii ø 25cm
5. R. keithii ø 80–90cm
6. R. pricei ø 80cm
7. R. tuan-mudae ø 50–70cm
8. R. cantleyi ø 30cm

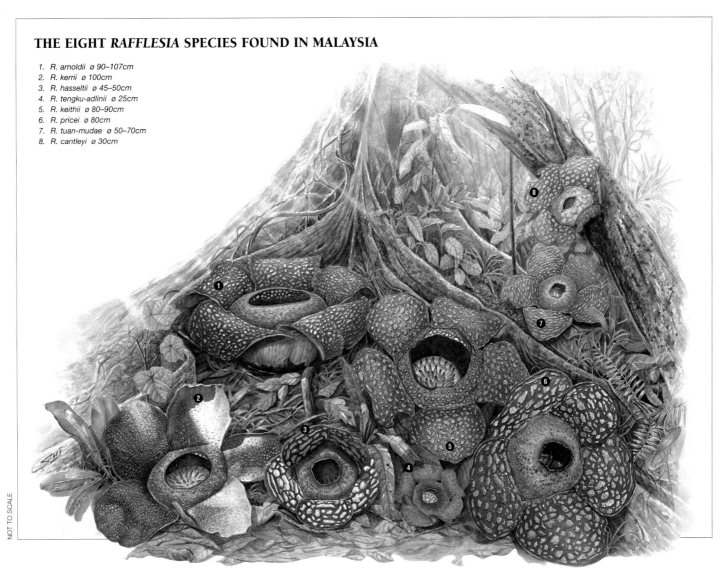

NOT TO SCALE

WHAT'S IN A NAME?

Many Malaysian places are named after trees found growing in the area. This table contains a sampling of some Malaysian towns and cities based on the names of common trees in the country.

- ALOR SETAR: The state capital of Kedah took its name from the *setar* tree (*Bouea macrophylla*) that belongs to the mango family. It is a native of the Malaysian forest.

- IPOH: The state capital of Perak in Malaysia is named after the *ipoh* tree (*Antiaris toxicaria*). As the Latin name implies, the tree contains toxic ingredients, which are used by the Orang Asli (aborigines) as blowpipe dart poison for hunting.

- MELAKA: There are several versions to the origin of the name of this historic state. One attributes it to the tree *Phyllanthus pectinata* that shaded the founder of Melaka, Parameswara. Another source attributes it to the fruit of another *Phyllanthus* species, *P. emblica*, locally known as the *pokok melaka*. The fruit is named after a Sanskrit word *amblaka* or *amalaka*, which describes its sour taste. The tree is widely planted for its fruits, which are used in cooking.

- KUALA KANGSAR: This royal town in the state of Perak is named after the *kangsar* (*Hibiscus floccosus*), a forest tree with red streaked flowers. *Kuala*,

which means confluence, is a common descriptive term for Malay towns that began as riverine settlements.

- PAHANG: The biggest state in Peninsular Malaysia is named after the *mahang* tree (*Macaranga* spp.). The *mahang* is a common tree found in secondary forest, which grows to fill the gap that occurs in the rainforest canopy. It needs full sunlight for at least part of the day to survive.

- PENANG: Penang obtained its name from the *pinang* tree (*Areca catechu*), which once grew in profusion on this island. The *pinang* is a palm tree, with bright orange fruits. It can be grown singly, in groups or in mixed planting.

Some flowering plants (Mycoheterotrophs) partner with fungi so that they can feed on dead matter. The fungi live in their cells and break down organic matter, which is then absorbed by the plant. They thrive in the cool, damp forest floor, amidst leaf litter and fungi. They look like they have been condemned as carcass-eaters; most species are pale, smooth and worm-like, with a short root system and no root hairs to absorb water and no stomata. Hence a life of complete dependence.

Some plants, however, appear totally opposed to this life choice. Instead of becoming resigned to their nutrient-deficient environments, a few flowering plants have come up with some of the most ingenious ways of feeding themselves. These are the much-admired insect eaters, who have evolved structurally to trap insects as food.

Malaysia is home to 47 species of such insectivorous flowering plants, which belong to totally unrelated families: bladderworts (*Utricularia*), sundews (*Drosera*) and pitcher plants (*Nepenthes*). They have little in common, in looks or location. Small and slender bladderworts can be found on water, on land or perched as epiphytes on damp and shady lowland and hill forests. Sundews are generally stemless, compact and hairy, growing on poor soils in beach, heath, swamp and montane forests. The handsome pitcher plant grows wild in lowland swamps and mountain ridges and summits. In Malaysia there are more than 30 species and many more natural hybrids; five pitcher plants are endemic to Peninsular

OPPOSITE: A woody root system snakes its way across the rainforest floor.

The stag's horn fern has two sets of leaves that perform different functions.

PITCHER PLANTS—NATURE'S INSECT TRAPS

The carnivorous pitcher plants are the marvel of the plant kingdom—the attractive pitchers lure insects with nectar-impregnated lips. The unsuspecting victims find themselves slipping down into the pitcher and eventually drowning in the digestive juices. The plant then laps up the nutrient-rich juices.

Nepenthes rafflesiara

Nepenthes tentaculata

NOT TO SCALE

Malaysia and 24 to Sabah and Sarawak. The largest pitcher plant in the world, the *N. rajah* can hold a litre of water in its pitcher and is endemic to Sabah, while the *N. northiana* is endemic to Sarawak, found only in the Bau limestone hills.

Each plant family has devised its own signature insect trap. The bladderwort trap is reminiscent of some of the most savage structures found in medieval castles. Everything here is reduced in size, but the operating principles are somewhat similar. An active trap, the bladderwort's trap door has bristles located at strategic points that sweep unsuspecting insects to the doorway, where they unfortunately activate trigger hairs… and voilà! The trap door opens, the insect is sucked in and the door slams shut. All over and done with in little more than 100th of a second. The plant is then ready to dine, digesting its prey with the help of secreted enzymes.

The sundew uses a combination of physical and chemical elements to trap its prey in a semi-active trap. The sticky leaves have two sets of tentacles—long ones on the edges brush the prey to the sticky centre, where it finds itself unable to escape. The

The elongated stem of a typical free-floating bladderwort (*Ultricularia* spp.).

LEFT: *Nepenthes villosa.* Exclusive to tropical rainforest, many species of *Nepenthes* pitcher plant are endemic to Malaysia.

RIGHT: *Nepenthes ampullaria.*

second set of shorter tentacles secrete digestive fluids once the prey is captured. The rapid rush of sweeping tentacles that immobilize the creature quickly overwhelms any last minute struggle by the prey. When the meal is over, the plant awaits its next victim.

The pitcher plant has an in-built trap—the leaf extends to produce a pitcher at the tip of the tendril. This is a passive trap, with insidious forbidden fruit. Unsuspecting insects are drawn to the sweet nectar in the pitcher, but alas, they slip off the waxy rim and fall down deep into the well. Chances of escape are nil and the insect eventually dies from drowning. Digestive juices in the bottom of pitcher help the plant absorb and digest its meal. Most pitcher plants have leaf lids to protect the pitcher from rain.

There is really no king in this close-knit kingdom of plants, where all life is finely networked to form an elaborate tapestry, often viewed as the mad muddle of the rainforest. Tug away one strand, and chances are many links will get undone. This is the way of the wilderness, where dependence is the rule of thumb, and nowhere is this better illustrated than in the relationship between the high and mighty dipterocarps and the lowly fungi. Fungi grow in profusion on the humid rainforest floor and are the life support systems of several forest giants, which bond with these forest midgets to survive in the shallow and poor soil conditions here. The survival mechanism is centred around their root systems that merge with one another to form a structure known as mycorrhiza, where the large tree

The *Lobelia* sp. with red berries, is a common creeper found along the edges of the forest.

PLANTS THAT ARE PRETTY, BUT POISONOUS

Some plants may be pretty to look at, but beneath their good looks lurks danger; they are poisonous when eaten. There are about 7,000 species of poisonous plants in the world, with most of them being found in hot, tropical rainforest environments. A 1976 report of the Department of Chemistry, Malaysia includes bitter cassava (*Manihot esculenta*) and *buah perah* (*Elateriospermum blume*) in its list of poisonous plants. After a meal of fried bitter cassava, two children, aged two and four, died in 1976; in a separate incident, two children in the same age group died after a meal of *buah perah*. Other toxic plants are the tuber root *Jatropha curcas*, *Sarcolobus globosus*, yellow oleander (*Thevetia peruviana*), amanita toxins (mushroom poison) and the castor oil plant (*Ricinus communis*).

Some of the most poisonous plants in Malaysia are used in native medicine.

For example, *Nerium oleander*, which contains toxic cardiac glycoside, is used to treat heart ailments. The dosage must be right; otherwise it can be fatal. Some measures are thus taken to remove the toxicity of some of these plants. The black nightshade (*Solanum nigrum*), which ranks as a favourite vegetable in Malaysia, is eaten in moderation because excessive amounts can cause headache and giddiness. *Buah perah* and bitter cassava should only be eaten after prolonged boiling.

Poisonous plants are classified according to the effects produced by their toxic principles such as glycosides, alkaloids and phytotoxins. They can cause a wide range of reactions that include external irritations such as eye infections (from sap of *Dieffenbachia picta*). *Digitalis lantana*, *N. oleander*, *T. peruviana* and milkweed (*Asclepia* spp.) are associated with nausea, vomiting, dizziness, lowered

NOT TO SCALE

The fruit of the *kecubung* (*Datura metel*) is poisonous.

pulse, irregular heart-beat and dilated pupils. Most lethal are *Abrus precatorius*, *J. curcas*, *R. communis* and *J. podagrica* which, if taken in excess, can cause severe gastrointestinal irritation, diarrhoea, dehydration and even death.

roots ride on fine fungal threads through the soil to bring water and scarce minerals to feed themselves. In return, the chlorophyll-less fungi are able to derive nutrients from their host. At least seven mycorrhizal associations including that between the main family of timber trees, Dipterocarpaceae, with the fungi Amanitaceae and Russulaceae, have been identified in the Malaysian rainforest. The *meranti tembaga* (*Shorea leprosula*) for example, partners with the *Amanita angustilamellata* and *Russula virescens*.

These tiny organisms wield tremendous power throughout the rainforest, both good and bad. They take on a variety of forms, from the invisible underground to colonies of vivid-hued mushrooms such as the *Hygrocybe* species that force their way up through the forest floor to disperse millions of dust-like spores to spread the species. Some glow like fibre-optic lights in the dark jungle night; many are barely visible. Some are short-lived while others such as the hard textured *Microporus affinis* last a long time.

Highly adaptable, they grow on water, soil and wood, with some such as the odorous stinkhorn fungus (*Dictyophora* spp.) growing on all three media.

OPPOSITE: Two majestic *tualang* trees (*Koompassia excelsa*) tower above a smaller *meranti* tree (*Shorea* sp.).

Huperzia phlegmaria, a club moss.

Fungi perform several roles: decomposing organic matter, recycling nutrients, and aerating the soil to sustain the continuous cycle of rainforest life. Many parasitic and saprophytic fungi live on soil, where their mycelia can often be seen rapidly advancing across the forest floor, decomposing and devouring leaf litter, assisted by armies of bacteria, insects and other small invertebrates. Water-based species such as chytrids and several members of the Ascomycota and Deuteromycota families decompose sewage and other organic matter. Some species also cause diseases in fish and humans. Wood is another favourite habitat, especially for the saprophytes, which feed on rotting wood.

Altogether, there are five groups of fungi, all found in Malaysia, which reproduce either by fragmentation, fission or budding, as with yeast, or by the production of spores that are dispersed by wind, water, insects and small mammals. Basidiomycota covers the range of colourful mushrooms, puffballs, stinkhorns, rusts and brackets. Oomycota, Zygomycota and Ascomycota fungi cause plant diseases and common food moulds. They are the farmers' curse, wreaking havoc on crops with their powdery mildew, leaf spots, rusts, tomato wilt, pod rots, root and heart rot. Some even infect human beings, causing athlete's foot, ringworm, barber's itch and respiratory diseases that also affect insects and birds. The good news is that some fungi can be used to control weeds, insects and plant diseases. Some are edible, delectable to animals ranging from arthropods and snails to large mammals such as the deer. Favourites for human consumption are paddy straw mushroom (*Volvariella* spp.), oyster mushroom (*Pleurotus* spp.), split gill mushroom (*Schizophyllum commune*) and termite mushroom (*Termitomyces* spp.). The fungus *Rhizopus oligosporus* is used to ferment soya beans to make *tempe*. Fungi's biggest contribution to humanity, however, comes from the Deuteromycota group, with its genus *Penicillium* providing the raw material for the antibiotic penicillin.

While fungi thrive on damp surfaces, water bodies such as ponds, rivers and lakes are fertile grounds for algae, commonly known as 'seaweed' or 'water moss' and more derogatorily as 'pond scum' and 'frog spittle'. They are an ancient group of plants, with a history that dates back more than 500 million years in the sea, before the advent of terrestrial plants. About 600 genera with 2,000 species of algae have been recorded in Malaysia. Occurring in a variety of aquatic environments—freshwater, seawater, clean water and polluted water, they grow suspended in water or on aquatic plants. Some algae thrive on rocks and stones by the banks of rivers, lakes, ponds and moist tree bark or attach themselves to hard-shelled animals such as molluscs.

Like the fungi, algae are life support systems, albeit in the water environment, where these photosynthesizing organisms are the primary producers of food and oxygen for aquatic plants and animals. They are also the spawning ground for several marine

OPPOSITE: Saprophytic bracket fungus (*Pycnoporus* sp.) growing on a rotten log.

A number of different fungi species with varied colours and shapes grow in Malaysia.

The colourful lichen, as seen on this tree trunk, grow slowly.

creatures. Unfortunately, algae suffer from a bad image, often accused of choking other aquatic life to death. This occurs in nutrient-rich polluted waters that tend to support large communities of some species of algae. The problem begins when they die; large algal communities tend to use up large supplies of oxygen during the decaying process, depriving other marine life of much-needed oxygen. Rivers are sometimes cleaned to remove marine life-threatening algae, which have the potential to cause the death of others sharing their habitat. Malaysian scientists studying the river system in Ulu Langat, Selangor have taken advantage of this peculiar algal characteristic; they use the presence of algae species to determine the water quality of rivers. High levels of *Meridion circulare* found in Sungai Gabai, Ulu Langat, Selangor were indicative of a clean river; while the profusion of several species of diatoms such as *Navicula cryptocephala*, *Gomphonema parvulum* and *Cymbella ventricosa* was used to classify the Sungai Langat as a polluted river.

While algae indicates water quality, lichen, another of the forest 'littlies', are air pollution indicators; they absorb atmospheric pollutants such as heavy metals and sulphur dioxide, and are killed when exposed to them over long periods. Found mainly in cooler, less humid and moist highland areas, lichen are the offspring of fungi-algae unions, or more precisely, they are borne out of the symbiotic relationship between the fungal threads called hyphae and a colony of microscopic, green or green-blue algae. The result is the lichen, which bear no resemblance to either 'parent' and behaves as an entity in its own right. Lichen are simple flora, with no true roots, stems or leaves; they consist

With 185,000 known species of fauna and 12,500 species of flowering plants, Malaysia ranks as one of the twelve 'mega-diverse' countries.

of two parts—the thallus and spore-containing ascocarps or fruits. On average, they grow only a few millimetres a year, with the quicker *Peltigera* recording up to three centimetres a year. They, however, compensate this with their hardiness and their long lives, with the *Usnea* eventually reaching a respectable two metres or more. Lichen prefer to grow on smooth, sunny and moist surfaces. Foliose lichen such as the *Parmotrema* appear as flattened leafy sheets, creeping across rocks, bark or hard-shelled molluscs; fruticose lichen such as *Usnea, Ramalina* and *Hetereodermia* drip as bushy beards from the tips of branches; crustose lichen such as *Chrysothrix* appear as patches on a variety of stable surfaces.

The lichen's highland habitat is shared by another small forest plant—the bryophyte, the simplest of all terrestrial plants. It grows no more than two centimetres in damp and shady groves above 1500 metres. More than 11 per cent of the world's 16,000 species are found in Malaysian highlands, with Mount Kinabalu alone housing 1,000 species or six per cent of the world total. This is the eerie world of the misty mossy forest, where bryophytes such as the *Sphagnum* species form a thick

Johannesteijsmannia magnifica, a splendid fan palm, is commonly found in hill dipterocarp forests.

green blanket across vast tracts of the forest floor while liverworts, hornworts and mosses drape around tree trunks and branches. The inconspicuous *Corybas* orchid piggybacks on bryophytes and several other small animals find refuge in them.

These are the ways of the wilderness, where plants have their in-house systems to check and balance their numbers in the rainforest environment. Dipterocarps, for example, occupy large spaces, making it impossible for all their saplings to mature into full-grown trees. There are also other culling processes in place, with death from pests and disease, bad weather and predatory plants, the primary causes of mortality. Every subject in the plant kingdom has its clearly defined job function that operates in a relatively flat organizational structure. Coup d'état is uncommon, and is rarely the result of other ambitious plants. The balance, however, is only tipped by long-term climatic changes and, in the shorter term, human intervention. Indeed, rainforest dynamics have inspired references to the 'human jungle' and 'concrete jungle' in deference to human life imitating that in the plant kingdom.

CHAPTER FOUR

ANIMALS OF THE RAINFOREST

The richness of rainforest flora is matched by a corresponding richness of fauna. The Malaysian rainforest is home to many endemic species: 40 endemic mammals, almost 30 endemic birds and a vast assemblage of unique aquatic life. One of the rarest endemic mammals is Hose's pygmy flying squirrel (*Petaurillus hosei*), a tiny nine-centimetre long animal. Then there are birds like the Kinabalu serpent-eagle (*Spilornis kinabaluensis*), the mountain peacock pheasant (*Polyplectron inopinatum*) and Malayan whistling thrush (*Myophorus robinsoni*) and fishes such as the Tioman cave loach (*Sundoreonectes tiomanensis*), freshwater stingray and the blackwater fish which has adapted itself to the waters of peatswamps.

Parallels between the plant and animal kingdoms can be traced back to their common history of evolution, marked by successive periods of global freezing and warming. The final warming caused sea levels to rise and parts of continental Asia eventually rose up as independent islands and peninsulas, collectively known as Sundaland, to which Malaysia belongs. The warmer climate was conducive for the growth of tropical rainforest, which established itself as the dominant vegetation. Cool climate vegetation receded to higher altitudes while savannah grasslands disappeared into obscurity. The land area, too, had shrunk, and terrestrial plants and animals found themselves having to adapt to these changed circumstances.

Isolated, they developed their own identity and, in a climate of higher temperatures, higher humidity and higher rainfall all year round, flora thrived. So did many animals; they were spoilt for choice in the multitude of habitats available amidst the rainforest flora. While feeding on plants that were adapting to the changing conditions, many animals also underwent changes in their own genetic make-up, causing some features to become more prominent while others receded from lack of use. This is best demonstrated in the size of the teeth. In the orang utan (*Pongo pygmaeus*), the lateral incisors and rear molars are much smaller than before; in two species of forest rats, the third and last molar have diminished in size; while some Sundaland rodent species have suffered a complete loss of rear molars.

The crested serpent-eagle (*Spilornis cheela*) ranges from lowlands to highlands and feeds mainly on snakes.

OPPOSITE: The orang utan is indigenous to the islands of Borneo and Sumatra.

LEFT TO RIGHT: A juvenile Wagler's pit viper (*Tropidolaemus wagleri*). These snakes are best-known as the main residents at Penang's Snake Temple.

The male atlas beetle (*Chalcosoma atlas*), one of Malaysia's large scarab beetles, has three horns, two on top and one below.

The Agamid lizard (*Calotes* sp.) is a semi-arboreal reptile found throughout the Malaysian rainforest.

The Malayan sun bear (*Helarctos malayanus*) often scales the tall *tualang* (*Koompassia excelsa*) tree to reach its favourite food—honey.

In the closed rainforest environment, plants found themselves having to grow skywards for sunlight. The rainforest thus distinguished itself with its tall and mighty trees, best represented by 60-metre high dipterocarps, which account for most of the forest cover in Malaysia. In contrast, many animals, especially large mammals, either disappeared or shrank in size. Hoofed animals that once grazed the grasslands which stretched across Sundaland found themselves disadvantaged. Grassland residents such as hyenas and hares are no longer found here, while the sabre-tooth cat and southern mammoth became extinct. The large Javan or one-horned rhinoceros (*Rhinoceros sondaicus*), Malayan tapir (*Tapirus indicus*) and red dog (*Cuon alpinus*), meanwhile, completely disappeared from Borneo.

Fossil remains indicate that Malaysian rainforest mammals are dwarf versions of their ancestors. The elephant is two-thirds the size of its ancestor, the southern mammoth (*Elephas* (*Archidiskodon*) *planifrons*), while the two-horned Sumatran rhinoceros (*Dicerorhinus sumatrensis*) has evolved into a shorter, dumpier form. Wild cattle, pigs and even that darling of the Malaysian jungle, the orang utan, are today smaller than the original. Indeed, Malaysian elephants, rhinoceroses, tigers and bears are the smallest members of their kind in the world. The Malayan sun bear (*Helarctos malayanus*) or honey bear is the smallest of the world's seven bears. The Asian elephant (*Elephas maximus*), found mainly in the national parks, is also smaller than the African elephant (*Loxodonta africana*).

Several scientific reasons have been put forward to explain this, largely viewed as the ultimate tribute to the adaptive skill of some animals. Large animals tend to overheat in hot, humid climates; so being small makes life easier. In dry heat, they can cool themselves by losing water through sweating. But sweating only makes things worse in the heavily saturated air of the humid tropical rainforest. The rainforest mammals coping skills vary.

Big cats such as the tiger, panther and leopard are nocturnal, preferring to move about in the cool of the night or early hours of the morning; rhinoceroses wallow in muddy pools on breezy hillsides; tapirs dive into the river; while deer and elephants lurk in the deep shade of the dense rainforest.

Even in undisturbed conditions, large animals are relatively scarce in the Malaysian rainforest. The moist and humid rainforest is a hotbed of parasites, predators and bacteria that keep in check the number of large mammals. In fact, rainforest mammals are greatly outnumbered by teeming populations of smaller life forms such as birds, reptiles, amphibians, aquatic animals and an impressive variety of other creepy-crawlies. There are 35 species of bees, about 140 species of land snakes, hundreds of spiders, beetles, ants, bugs, flies, mosquitoes, scorpions, centipedes, millipedes and an assortment of parasites. Many are harmless, but a few have the potency to bring powerful beasts to their knees, especially when they attack en masse, as do hornets and wasps, or more insidiously like worms, ticks, mites and other parasites.

Moreover, the rainforest is a poor source of food for herbivores such as elephants, seladang, deer and cattle, which require massive quantities of succulent herbage.

A praying mantis (Mantodea) struggles to escape the carnivorous pitcher plant (*Nepenthes* sp.).

*'Duduk seperti kucing,
melompat seperti harimau.'*
To sit like a cat and leap like a tiger.

MALAY PROVERB REFERRING
TO A BRAVE MAN.

The Malaysian tiger (*Panthera tigris corbetti*), the largest cat in the country.

The tall difficult-to-reach canopies and under-storey of slow-growing woody saplings and spiny palms are not the best of buffet spreads. To make matters worse, many plants are indigestible or contain toxic chemicals. Put simply, rainforest conditions are not ideal to support great numbers of large herbivores needing huge quantities of vegetable matter or extensive home ranges. Although few in number, many of the large mammals, however, occupy a special place in the Malaysian national psyche, both culturally as well as in its wildlife conservation efforts.

The *harimau* or Malaysian tiger *(Panthera tigris corbetti)* is the national animal of the Federation, featured in the nation's coat of arms. This immensely powerful beast is the largest of Malaysian cats and the most formidable of carnivores. The adult male, with an average length of 2.6 metres and weighing up to 150 kilograms, is capable of killing buffalo, and attacks on elephants are not unknown. Its main prey is the prolific wild pig *(Sus scrofa)* and the bearded pig *(S. barbatus)*. There are also cases of rogue tigers in forest fringes that prey on livestock, and man-eaters have been recorded. These nocturnal animals are found in primary and secondary forests of northeastern Peninsular Malaysia, where they are often found roaming alone in their respective territories of at least 20 square kilometres each. Protected under the Wildlife Protection Act 1972, captured tigers are sent to the Melaka Zoo, where there is a breeding programme.

The tiger, a totally protected animal, appears on Malaysia's coat of arms.

OPPOSITE: The common brown-throated sunbird (*Anthreptes malacensis*), feeding its young on the wing.

THE EYE IN THE SKY

How do you keep an eye on an elephant? With a big eye in the sky—the satellite.

Malaysia's Department of Wildlife and National Parks (DWNP), in collaboration with the Smithsonian Institution Conservation and Research Centre, has set up the Malaysian Elephant Satellite Tracking Programme to evaluate the effectiveness of its elephant translocation efforts.

DWNP has captured and translocated 425 elephants since 1974. Most of these animals, which were displaced from their natural habitats by land development for agriculture and human settlement, had become threats to crops and homes, especially those on forest fringes.

Satellite tracking is considered the best method of tracking elephant movements as ground tracking telemetry is unreliable in the hilly terrain and dense foliage of the rainforest. A transmitter attached to the elephant beams signals to satellites, which

The Asian elephant (*Elephas maximus*) is a totally protected animal.

in turn relay signals to earth stations that compute the animal's position.

In 1995, a female affectionately dubbed Mek Penawar became the first Asian elephant to be fitted with a transmitter as part of the translocation exercise. Her movements were then monitored, and her transmitter emitted

signals until 29 August 1996. After analysis, the readings showed that she ranged an astonishing 7,000 square kilometres in just ten and a half months!

The second 'wired' elephant to be released was a male, Abang Ramadan, in February 1996. Although he was released at the same spot as Mek Penawar, he ranged only 350 square kilometres in six months. More than three and a half years passed before a third elephant, Mek Boh, with a new-generation transmitter collar, was released at the same spot as the other two, together with her teenaged male calf.

Although tracking is expensive—a year's tracking bill comes up to about RM14,000 (US$3,700)—it is considered useful in providing comprehensive answers to the question of what makes translocated elephants go where they go and also in offering more insights into elephant behaviour and habits in the rainforest.

The infant of the noctural Malayan pangolin or scaly anteater (*Manis javanica*) tends to cling to the base of its mother's tail.

Since the arrival of the first tiger in 1981, more than 30 cubs have been born in captivity, some of whom have become part of breeding programmes of other local and foreign zoos. Strict enforcement laws have resulted in steady growth of the tiger population in their natural habitat; from 300 in 1976 to 600 in 1995. This makes Malaysia a major conservation area for tigers, with 12 per cent of the world tiger population of 5000. After India, Malaysia is believed to have the second largest tiger population in the world.

Strict enforcement has also resulted in the increase in the population of wild elephants from below 1,000 in the mid-1970s to 1,500 in 1999. Protected by counteracting the illegal trade in ivory, elephants are the largest of all land animals. The tusk, from which ivory is obtained, is really a protruding incisor tooth, and the molar of the elephant reflects its age. In Peninsular Malaysia, elephants are indigenous but they are believed to have been introduced into Borneo, initially as domesticated animals that were presented as gifts to the Sultan of Sulu by the East India Company in 1750. Weighing between 3,000–4,000 kilograms, the daily diet of these herbivores consists of approximately 250 kilograms of vegetation a day. Those found on forest fringes have no qualms about trampling through crops and digging up roots and tubers to feed themselves. Like tigers, elephants require large roaming grounds and are best confined to large forest reserves.

Another magnificent beast of the rainforest is the seladang (*Bos gaurus*), the second largest mammal in Malaysia and once a trophy of colonial hunters. These massive 900-kilogram wild cattle stand close to two metres high and have white stockinged legs. They have a prominent white forehead, from which a pair of horns sweep back in a curve. Looking more fearsome than they behave, these gregarious creatures move about in

Weighing up to 900 kilograms, the second largest mammal in Malaysia is the formidable seladang (*Bos gaurus*).

herds in the lowlands, preferring the cool of the forest cover in the heat of the day and the open clearings and forest fringes by night. But they are no farmer's friend, since the herds tend to ride roughshod over crops when feeding. Bullfights are part of the rites of passage for young males seeking to establish their domination of the herd by driving out the incumbent.

The seladang is listed as an endangered animal by the International Union for Conservation of Nature and Natural Resources (IUCN) Red Data Book, the US Fish and Wildlife Service and the Convention on International Trade in Endangered Species (CITES). Its population stands at between 300–400, mainly in Kedah, Perak, Johor, Pahang, Terengganu and Kelantan. The seladang breeding programme that was started in 1982 in Pahang's Krau Wildlife Reserve conserves the captured animals that are bred and releases the calves into their natural habitat.

ADULT MALAYAN TAPIR AND BABY

The Malayan tapir (*Tapirus indicus*) is a master of camouflage—its dark areas blend with trees and its light areas blend with filtered light. The baby is differently coloured, with tawny streaks and spots to simulate the light-dappled leaves on the forest floor.

NOT TO SCALE

The Malayan tapir (*Tapirus indicus*) is a curious-looking animal. Measuring two metres long, it looks like a slightly small, snub-faced rhino with black-and-white colouration. Its black face and body and white hind area make it conspicuous in the zoo; but this is precisely what makes it inconspicuous in the jungle. Found only in Peninsular Malaysia and nocturnal by nature, they are generally solitary creatures though they have been seen in twos and threes. When the tapir roams across the jungle, its colouring camouflages its body within the alternating shade and light of the forest. The tapir produces only one offspring, and the baby is brown with tawny spots and streaks. Adult tapirs prefer to rest in open spaces, especially by the river, where they enjoy diving. There is only one other region where tapirs are found—South America, where three species exist, all with plain coloured adults. In comparison, the Malayan tapir is exotic and much sought-after by zoos around the world, which, unfortunately, also makes this totally protected animal the target of illegal wildlife traders.

The Malaysian Nature Society logo features the Malayan tapir.

NEXT PAGE: The immensely powerful tiger.

The sambar deer (*Cervus unicolor*) is fond of nibbling the bark of rubber trees.

Another victim of poaching is the Sumatran rhinoceros (*Dicerorhinus sumatrensis*), the most endangered animal in Malaysia. It is also the smallest and most primitive of the five surviving rhinoceros species (two in Africa and three in Asia). Found mainly in lowland dipterocarp forests, this hoofed animal can be easily detected because of its appearance and well-defined walking trail. It has two horns, slit eyes, folds around the trunk and brown-grey hide. An adult weighs up to 500–750 kilograms.

The penalty for illegal ownership or harming this totally protected animal is a possible five-year jail sentence in addition to a fine. But the high commercial value for rhinoceros products, believed by Asians as having medicinal properties, continues to be a draw card. Rhinoceros horn is a highly desired aphrodisiac and is also believed to reduce fever; the hide is said to cure skin diseases and the entrails relieve constipation. It is estimated that there are altogether between 800–1,000 Sumatran rhinoceroses left in Myanmar, Thailand, Sumatra and Malaysia. Of this, 150–220 are found in Malaysia.

The Malaysian rainforest is home to several species of deer, the largest being the *rusa* or sambar deer (*Cervus unicolor*). Sambar range in colouring from pale to dark brown and their fawns have faint spots at birth. Adult males have antlers. Their diet consists mainly of grasses, plant shoots, leaves of shrubs and fruit that has fallen to the forest floor. Sambar deer are occasionally a nuisance to farmers and commercial agriculture as they invade plantations to nibble on young plants.

The Indian muntjak (*Muntiacus muntjak*), which reaches up to 55 centimetres at the shoulder, is not as large as the sambar which can be as tall as 1.5 metres; but it has similar antlers, and its young is spotted as well. As they grow older, the deer lose the spots. The muntjak is often referred to as the 'barking deer' because

THE SUMATRAN RHINOCEROS

The Department of Wildlife and National Parks Malaysia began a rhinoceros breeding programme in 1984. Six years later Sungai Dusun Wildlife Conservation Centre, Ulu Bernam, Selangor, became the main centre for captive breeding of the endangered Sumatran rhinoceros. Currently the centre has six rhinoceros in captivity, four females and two males. Another three rhinos—one male and two female have been bred in the Melaka Zoo; unfortunately, several attempts to mate them have failed. The Global Environment Facility, jointly operated by United Nations Development Programme, United Nations Environment Programme and the World Bank, has allocated RM3.8 million (USD1 million) for Malaysia's programme to conserve the Sumatran rhinoceros.

The Sumatran rhinoceros escapes the heat of the day by wallowing in mud holes.

MALAYSIA'S DEER AND MOUSE DEER

There are vast differences in the size and weight of the Malaysian deer and mouse deer, the smaller being the lesser mouse deer at two kilograms and the greater mouse deer at 4.5 kilograms. The barking deer or muntjak can weigh up to 20 kilograms while the sambar deer is the largest, reaching weights of up to 200 kilograms.

1. Sambar deer (*Cervus unicolor*)
2. Muntjak (*Muntiacus muntjak*)
3. Lesser mouse deer (*Tragulus javanicus*)
4. Greater mouse deer (*Tragulus napu*)

INSET: The mouse deer are shy, fleet-footed animals.

it makes loud barking noises to scare away predators. It feeds on fruits, leaves and herbs and can be found in hill and mountain ranges, unlike the sambar, which prefers deeper forest cover.

The mouse deer (Tragulidae) is often the hero of folk tales where its cunning gets the better of larger animals. It comes in two sizes: lesser (*Tragulus javanicus*) and greater (*Tragulus napu*). They are both tiny nocturnal forest dwellers that have slender hooves but no antlers, and are also referred to as chevrotains, the world's smallest hoofed animals. Both feed on fallen fruit, plant shoots and fungi, and live in primary and secondary jungle. There are only four species of chevrotain in the world. Besides the greater and lesser mouse deer, the others are the African water chevrotain (*Hyemoschus aquaticus*) and the Indian chevrotain (*Moschiola meminna*).

The bravery of the mouse deer, referred to as *Sang Kancil* in local folk tales, reputedly so impressed Sumatran prince, Parameswara, that he decided to found a

'Seperti rusa masuk kampung.'
Like a deer which enters a village.

MALAY PROVERB USING THE DEER AS A
COMPARISON TO A PERSON SHY AND
AWKWARD IN AN UNUSUAL SETTING.

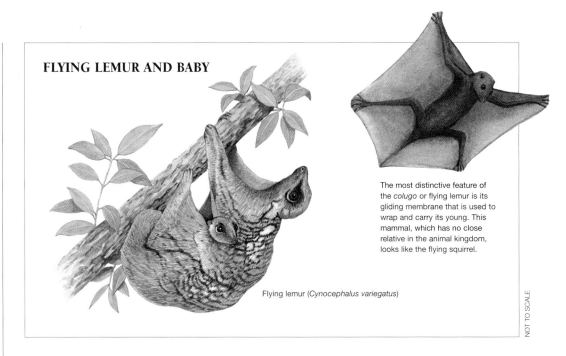

FLYING LEMUR AND BABY

The most distinctive feature of the *colugo* or flying lemur is its gliding membrane that is used to wrap and carry its young. This mammal, which has no close relative in the animal kingdom, looks like the flying squirrel.

Flying lemur (*Cynocephalus variegatus*)

NOT TO SCALE

ABOVE: Large communities of the common *kera* or long-tailed macaque (*Macaca fascicularis*) are found in urban reserves.

The orang utan (*Pongo pygmaeus*) is one of two kinds of apes found in Asia; the other is the gibbon.

settlement where the doughty little animal had royally routed his dogs. The settlement went on to become Melaka, one of the most famous ports in the Far East. The mouse deer is featured on the Melaka state emblem.

While the majority of large mammals are seldom seen or heard, primates can often be seen and heard. The most evolved of animals, they occupy the highest order of the animal kingdom. They are believed to have their origins in some climbing member of the Scandentia, something like a tree shrew, and the broad stages of primate evolution as seen in the living fauna of the Malaysian rainforest are without parallel. The stages are represented in the lemur-like slow loris and western tarsier, monkeys, gibbons, apes, and finally, man.

The arboreal *kongkang* or slow loris (*Nycticebus coucang*) is a grey, saucer-eyed, furry and cuddly 30 centimetre-long bundle that sleeps all day and forages for insects, lizards and fruits at night. It climbs slowly, hence its name. The *kera hantu* or western tarsier (*Tarsius bancanus*), a nocturnal primate, has large ears and saucer-like eyes. More evolved than the slow loris, it can make powerful frog-like standing jumps and has a dry nose like a monkey or man, which places it above the slow loris on the evolution ladder.

Monkeys are a more advanced lot and live in small communities. They are larger, live longer and are good climbers, often scampering across kilometres of the rainforest. There are three groups of monkey, all omnivorous—the macaques, the langurs or leaf monkeys and the distinctive proboscis monkey of Sabah and Sarawak.

The long-tailed macaque (*Macaca fascicularis*) is the most common primate in Malaysia. One-third of its 60-centimetre length is in its long, half erect and curved tail;

thus its name. It moves about in groups of 8–40. They are good swimmers, often hunting for crabs in mangrove swamps and beaches. Although protected by law, they are sometimes kept as pets, some living for as long as 20 years. Prior to the 1980s, long-tailed macaques were exported to laboratories for medical experiments but this practice has since been abandoned given their recent 'protected' status. The pig-tailed macaque (*Macaca nemestrina*) is more thickset and darker, and less sociable. It prefers a solitary existence or moves in small groups, on the ground rather than off the ground. It is, nonetheless, a good climber and is best known for its vocation as a coconut picker. One Singapore botanist even trained some to pick and fling down leaves, flowers and fruits from selected trees, declaring he could not have written his book on Malayan trees if not for their help!

Leaf monkeys (*Presbytis* spp.) are strict vegetarians that live high up in the trees. A little larger and shaggier than the long-tailed macaque, they distinguish themselves with their exceptionally long tails—1.5 times their body length! All leaf monkeys are gregarious, and vary in colouring and habitat. There are several species, from the silvered leaf monkey (*P. cristata*) found along the west coast of Peninsular Malaysia and coastal Sabah and Sarawak to the dusky leaf monkey (*P. obscura*), also known as the spectacled leaf monkey, in the lowland and hill forests of the Peninsula, to the most common of them all—the banded leaf monkey (*P. melalophos*) in the interior forests of the Peninsula. Then there is the Hose's langur or grey leaf monkey (*P. hosei*) and the red leaf monkey (*P. rubicunda*) that are found only in Sabah and Sarawak, while the white-fronted leaf monkey (*P. frontata*) is endemic to central Sarawak.

The *orang Belanda* or proboscis monkey (*Nasalis larvatus*) is another vegetarian, feeding almost entirely on the leaves of the *Sonneratia* tree. Strong swimmers, they can be seen diving into the water from high branches in the peatswamps of Sabah, Sarawak and also in Kalimantan. The adult male is an odd-looking specimen, with reddish fur, a large, droopy nose (hence its name), and a white ruff around its neck. In 1885 William T. Hornaday, a hunter and naturalist observed: '*As the name would imply, the most striking feature of the proboscis monkey is its nose. In old male specimens, this organ reaches its grandest proportions, and is truly enormous in length, breadth and thickness. It hangs from the face like – well, totally unlike anything else in the world, coming quite below the lowest point of the chin, shaped like a pear except for*

The banded leaf monkey (*Presbytis melalophos*), the most common of the six leaf monkeys, is found mainly in the interior forests of Peninsular Malaysia.

'Seperti kera dapat canggung.'
Like an ape which has caught
hold of a snag.

MALAY PROVERB MEANING LIKE A
FOOL CLINGING TO BAD ADVICE.

The herbivorous proboscis monkey is
found only in the coastal swamps of
Borneo. Above: Female. Below: Male.

THE NOSEY MONKEY

Its local name, *orang Belanda* (Dutchman) is probably indicative of what the natives thought of Caucasian features. The adult male proboscis monkey (*Nasalis larvatus*) has a very prominent drooping nose and a red-skinned face—rather like a sunburned European. The female proboscis, in contrast to the male, has an upturned nose. Both sexes have grey-reddish, brown-orange fur. Infant proboscis monkeys reportedly have dark blue faces.

Confined exclusively to East Malaysia, the proboscis monkey congregates in groups along river banks and swampland. They are gregarious and sociable, with smaller groups often joining larger ones. They are noisy, having a wide range of calls: honks, groans, squeals and roars. Believed to have once been leaf monkeys that have completely adapted to living in swampy areas like forests on river banks, mangrove forests, mixed mangrove and nipa forest; proboscis monkeys feed on leaves, shoots, fruits and seeds. They are good swimmers, and have been observed frequently diving into the water from riverside trees.

Research has shown that proboscis monkeys obtain energy from the large amounts of cellulose they consume. However, what research does NOT show is the reason for that large red nose, which straightens out when the proboscis monkey honks!

a furrow down the middle and a contracted septum, which causes the organ to terminate in two points. It is broadest at the middle of the free portion instead of at the base.'

Monkeys and apes are often confused; but there are clear differences. Monkeys have tails, while apes do not. Monkeys move on all fours, even when climbing while apes use only two limbs, when walking or swinging from branch to branch using their arms in a process called brachiation. Apes also have highly developed brains and are more intelligent than monkeys. Not surprisingly, apes are further up the evolution chain and are man's closest relative in the animal kingdom. There are four apes in the world—the chimpanzee and gorilla of Africa and the gibbon and orang utan of Asia. Both Asia's apes are found in Malaysia, where they are protected species.

Gibbons are among the noisiest and most visible of rainforest denizens. Territorial animals, they live in clearly demarcated residential areas, and move about in small groups foraging for fruits, leaves and insects on the forest canopy, seldom to descend. The largest of them all is the all-black, one-metre tall siamang (*Hylobates syndactylus*), which lives in the interior forests of Perak, Kelantan, Pahang and Negeri Sembilan.

Unlike many other monkeys, the
proboscis monkey is not inhibited
by water and is known to dive into
rivers, swimming across easily.

NOT TO SCALE

PRIMATE MOVEMENT

Primates are arboreal mammals whose limbs have adapted for grasping and climbing. They also have sharp vision to judge distances, an essential skill when climbing.

1. White-handed gibbon (*Hylobates lar*)
2. Orang utan (*Pongo pygmaeus*)
3. Western tarsier (*Tarsius bancanus*)
4. Slow loris (*Nycticebus coucang*)
5. Dusky leaf monkey (*Presbytis obscura*)
6. Pig-tailed macaque (*Macaca nemestrina*)

NOT TO SCALE

JUNGLE MAN'S SANCTUARY

There's something inimitably endearing about the orang utan (*Pongo pygmaeus*), the Malay word meaning 'man of the jungle.' Noted naturalist and writer, Gerald Durrell, once sold a very expensive animal conservation idea to no less than Princess Grace of Monaco, using a picture of a baby orang utan—or so the story goes.

The orang utan's wide-eyed innocence stops people in their tracks, which is just as well because as Asia's only great ape representative, it is classified as a totally protected species—and the more people sympathize with its plight, the better its chances of being removed from the list of totally protected animals.

Because of its totally protected status, efforts to conserve the species have been in place since the early 1960s. At the forefront in the work of conservation and rehabilitation of the orang utan is the Sepilok

Rehabilitation Centre, on the east coast of Sabah. At Sepilok, young orang utan, which have lost their mothers—either through poaching or disease, are cared for until they are old enough to be returned to the forest. They are encouraged to develop orang utan behaviour like climbing and building nests, and are gradually exposed to other orang utans and life in the wild.

Another rehabilitation centre has since been established in Semenggoh, Sarawak, but Sepilok is a conservation success story that draws thousands of visitors each year. Visitors are cautioned not to wear jewellery or carry items likely to distract its residents. Orang utan are inquisitive creatures that will rifle through bags

The orang utan at the rehabilitation centre undergo training to help them prepare to return to the jungle.

and take away watches and cameras—to the consternation of the owners of such articles—and then gaily abandon the items to the forest!

Their deep, booming voices resound across the rainforest, making them the loudest of gibbons. The more common *wa-wa* or white-handed gibbon (*Hylobates lar*) usually has black to buff to cream fur, with white hands and feet and is a common resident of the lowland forest. Family ties are strong among them. Unmated gibbons, however, tend to live solitary bachelor lives, away from raucous family fun. Less common is the agile gibbon (*Hylobates agilis*), which is restricted to the north of the Peninsula and the Bornean gibbon (*Hylobates muelleri*) that is found only in the lowland and hill forests of Sabah and Sarawak.

The siamang (*Hylobates syndactylus*) is found only in the hills of Peninsular Malaysia. This gibbon is known for its dark, brooding looks and booming voice.

The only great ape of Asia is the lovable orang utan (*Pongo pygmaeus*), found only in the lowland forests of Borneo and Sumatra. With the bulk of a human being, the adult female weighs between 35–50 kilograms. The male can be as heavy as 100 kilograms and may grow up to 1.4 metres. Given their size and weight, they do not have the agility of gibbons; instead they hang on branches and move about upright, with their long arms moving from side to side—just like Man! The male leads a bachelor's life, meeting the female for procreation. He then returns to his solitary existence, while she raises the family—alone. Strong mother-child bonding is fostered, with the child weaned when it is two years old, after which it is taught living skills. If abandoned at this stage, the young orang utan is most likely to die. It matures at around eight years old, when it begins to live independently. Females then try to mate again to raise another child. Orang utans are known to live up to 40 years of age.

These arboreal mammals are the only primates to build a nest as their home, a platform of interwoven branches, where they sleep at night. They are known to change their 'sheets' daily or even several times a day, collecting a fresh batch of branches for their nests. They feed on bark, leaves, flowers, fruit and insects and their greatest enemies are pythons (*Python* spp.) and the clouded leopard (*Neofelis nebulosa*), which prey on young orang utans. A totally protected species, the penalty for hunting, capturing or killing an orang utan is a RM30,000 fine (US$8,000) or a two-year jail term. There are about 35,000 orang utans in Borneo and Sumatra, giving the species a healthy gene pool for survival.

As night falls, small dark shapes detach themselves from rock formations within caves, drop off shadowy branches of tall trees, and issue from the eaves of houses. Bats—the only mammals that can really fly, come alive at night. Their wings are actually membranes of skin between the forelimbs and elongated fingers.

There are more than 80 species of bats in Malaysia, making them the most species-rich group of mammals, and the most successful at adapting to habitats. All are night flyers, and can be classified as either fruit-eating (Megachiroptera) or insect-eating (Microchiroptera). An exception to this rule seems to be the false vampire bat (*Megaderma lyra*), a rather large bat which has been known to eat small birds and smaller bats that cross its path.

At dusk, a little ripple goes through the colonies; the bats are stirring, swooping out of their roosting places in droves, ready for a nocturnal hunt that involves some of the most sophisticated navigational equipment ever to be developed naturally. The largest of all bats, *Pteropus vampyrus*, or flying foxes, have a wingspan of up to 1.5 metres and the smallest, of the genus *Tylonycteris*, may have bodies only four centimetres long.

MANGROVE MONKEYS

The silvered leaf monkey and dusky leaf monkey share a common feature with the proboscis monkey: all consume swamp vegetation.

1. Proboscis monkey (*Nasalis larvatus*)
2. Silvered leaf monkey (*Presbytis cristata*)
3. Dusky leaf monkey (*Presbytis obscura*)

NOT TO SCALE

BATS

The features of fruit bats and insectivorous bats are quite different. Fruit bats have large eyes and small ears and have muzzles rather than the snout-like noses of insectivorous bats which have 'noseleaves', layers of skin lined with sensitive hairs that help detect danger. Fruit bats also have a claw on their second digit and an under-developed membrane between their legs. They may have a short tail or no tail at all.

Fruit bat

Insectivorous bat

NOT TO SCALE

Bats use their feet to grip their perch, whether in a cave or a tree. Bats live together in large colonies and use echolocation (radar system using vibrations) to guide their way in the dark.

Insect-eating bats navigate and hunt by echolocation, a process in which the bat issues ultrasonic pulses (which register off the scale of human hearing) or sound waves. These sound waves are deflected off objects around the bat, which can expertly interpret the distance of the objects—like flying insects, which it eats on the wing—and avoid or hunt them down accordingly.

Because they have such a highly developed sense of hearing, their other senses are somewhat retarded when compared to those of other animals. However, they are not blind, regardless of the saying, 'As blind as a bat.' Some fruit bats have large eyes to assist them in dusk and dawn hunting.

Besides keeping the insect population under control, bats also perform integral functions of pollination and seed dispersal. Species like the cave fruit bat (*Eonycteris spelaea*) and hill long-tongued bat (*Macroglossus sobrinus*) collect pollen from the inflorescence of the plants they feed on and later brush it off on others. Because of the long distances they can cover from their roosting sites to their feeding grounds and back, bats disperse seeds from the fruit they ingest over a wide area. In addition, their droppings in caves and around large trees is a food source for smaller animals.

The Malaysian forest is a wonderland of birds, with 624 species, a third of them migrants on transit between the northern and southern hemisphere. The most flamboyant of them all are the hornbills (Bucerotiformes), with their enormous, often

OPPOSITE: Eagles feeding on fish are a common sight in coastal areas and the inland lakes of Malaysia.

reddish-yellow bill that is mounted by a 'horn' known as a casque. This contrasts sharply against its long, black and white plumage. Ten of the world's 54 species of hornbill are found at various altitudes in Malaysia. The *kenyalang* or rhinoceros hornbill (*Buceros rhinoceros*) is the state bird of Sarawak, which is often called the 'Land of Hornbills'. Carved wooden *kenyalang* are often used as talismen to keep enemies at bay. Hornbill feathers are used to decorate traditional attire while the casque is carved into earrings.

The nesting habits of the hornbill are unusual. They live mainly as couples or small groups. Using a hole in a tree for a nest, the female is sealed into the hole by the male using a mixture of clay, organic matter and its own droppings. This protects the female and any eggs from predators. The female will remain in the sealed nest throughout egg-laying, incubation and after the eggs have hatched; about a three month period. During this time the male feeds the female through a narrow slit in the seal.

The kingfisher is another common bird in the Malaysian forest. It is an attractive bird with brilliant aquamarine or royal blue plumage, large head, large bill, short tail and short legs. Noisy, solitary birds that live by the water, they can often be seen diving into the water for fish, crabs, tadpoles and aquatic insects or swooping down from tall trees preying on insects, lizards and arachnids. The common *raja udang* or kingfisher (*Alcedo atthis*) is a bird about 16 centimetres tall that lives near water, and even in forests at altitudes up to 1800 metres high. The most widely

Over 165 species of frogs and toads live in the Malaysian rainforest and wetlands.

The migratory harrier's (*Circus* spp.) favoured destination is the paddy field.

HORNBILLS

Malaysia has ten species of the 54 species of hornbills found throughout the world. Hornbills are also found in India, New Guinea, sub-Saharan Africa and the Solomon Islands.

1. Great hornbill (*Buceros bicornis*)
2. Plain-pouched hornbill (*Aceros subruficolis*)
3. Wreathed hornbill (*Aceros undulatus*)
4. Wrinkled hornbill (*Aceros corrugatus*)
5. Bushy-crested hornbill (*Anorrhinus galeritus*)
6. White-crowned hornbill (*Aceros comatus*)
7. Helmeted hornbill (*Buceros vigil*)
8. Oriental pied hornbill (*Anthracoceros albirostris*)
9. Rhinoceros hornbill (*Buceros rhinoceros*)
10. Black hornbill (*Anthracoceros malayanus*)

NOT TO SCALE

seen kingfisher, the *pekaka belukar* or white-breasted kingfisher (*Halcyon smyrnensis*) has brilliant aquamarine plumage and can be seen on electricity cables and dead branches in paddy fields and oil palm estates. Most unusual is the kingfisher's nest, a 0.5–one metre long hole along a steep riverbank, earth bank or termite mound. It builds its nest by ramming the bank with its powerful beak to loosen the soil. It uses its claws and bill to dig a tunnel, with a breeding chamber located at the far end.

The wetlands of Malaysia are a haven for water birds, with more than half of the 156 species being non-residents. Some stop over briefly, while others treat their visit as their long winter vacation. They have the physical attributes to live in waterlogged conditions. Shorebirds such as the sandpiper, swamphen and waterhen, have short legs and needle-like beaks. Herons, egrets and storks have long stilt-like legs to wade in water, probing for small fish, aquatic animals and insects with their long beaks.

The cattle egret (*Bubulcus ibis*) is often seen with cattle and buffaloes and feeds on insects.

The nocturnal *pucung kuak* or black-crowned night heron (*Nycticorax nycticorax*), a local resident, even feeds on rats and snakes. Most of the heron populations swell with the onset of northern winters, when large flocks flee the cold. All *bangau* (egrets) in Malaysia are migrants. These pure white birds change colour with the breeding season. Their faces turn bluish green, the bills turn from yellow to black and the thighs become a shade of green. They also develop two long plumes on the nape. The most common of them all is the cattle egret, often found perched on the backs of buffaloes and cattle in paddy fields and marshes. As a tribute to these visitors, the mast guard of the traditional fishing boats in Kelantan and Terengganu is called a *bangau*, and is often shaped in the design of the bird (*see p148*).

There are 41 birds of prey in Malaysia living in a variety of habitats, from wetlands to montane forests. Some are local residents, some migrants and a few stopover passengers en route to other destinations. They can be distinguished by their strong, hooked bills and powerful clawed feet—both used for clutching and ripping up their victims. Most of them are solitary birds or hunt in pairs. They prey on anything from tiny insects to full-size fowls and flying foxes. The most respected of them all is the *lang merah* or brahminy kite (*Haliastur indus*), which is revered by the Iban as the 'Singalang Burung', bird-god of war. This white and chestnut-coloured local can be spotted soaring gracefully above wetlands and villages, before it swoops down on its prey. It nests in mangrove trees.

MALAYSIA'S PHEASANTS AND JUNGLE FOWL

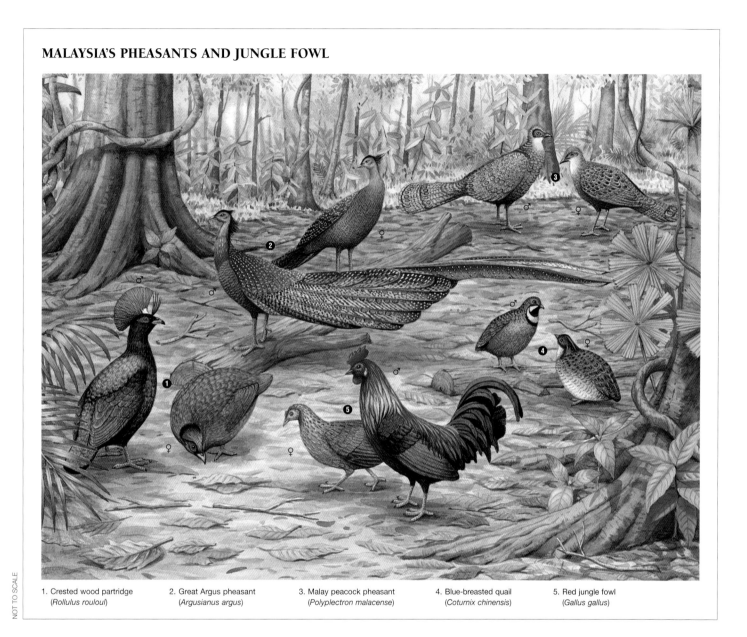

NOT TO SCALE

1. Crested wood partridge
   (*Rollulus rouloul*)

2. Great Argus pheasant
   (*Argusianus argus*)

3. Malay peacock pheasant
   (*Polyplectron malacense*)

4. Blue-breasted quail
   (*Coturnix chinensis*)

5. Red jungle fowl
   (*Gallus gallus*)

Hovering over paddy fields and oil palm plantations are the small *lang bahu hitam* or black-shouldered kites (*Elanus caeruleus*) that feed on mice, rats, snakes and grasshoppers. Just a little larger than doves, their piercing red eyes appear awesome against grey-black feathers. These kites share the sky with the *lang berjambul* or crested serpent-eagle (*Spilornis cheela*), which also tends to range over mountains. The *lang siput* or white-bellied sea-eagle (*Haliaeetus leucogaster*) lives close to the coast and waterways, where it swoops in on fish, turtles and flying foxes. The *lang lebah/madu* or crested honey buzzard (*Pernis ptilorhyncus*) breeds in Siberia, and stops over in Malaysia on its way to and back from the Sunda Islands where it spends winter. The migrants

Young tailor birds (*Orthotomus* sp.), which derive their common name from its neatly sewn nest.

arrive as jumbo-size flocks, with as many as 500 birds at any one time. Also following the same route and flock size is the *lang baza berjambul* or black baza (*Aviceda leuphotes*), with some choosing to terminate their journey in Malaysia. The *lang tiram* or osprey (*Pandion haliaetus*) parks itself near the sea, where it nests on cliffs or trees and only feeds on fish. Other winter visitors include the *lang barat* or marsh harrier (*Circus aeruginosus*) that prefers water-based locations.

The most significant bird in the world must surely be the *ayam hutan* or red jungle fowl (*Gallus gallus*). It packs a lot of importance into its 40–75 centimetre stature because of it lineage: it is the ancestor of the domestic chicken. The most common of Malaysian game birds, it is part of the ground crew that live close to the forest floor; it cannot fly. Like most members of the animal kingdom, the males are blessed with good looks, which they flaunt to attract a harem of plain looking females. The polygamous red jungle fowl cockerel is known to stray into the turf of domestic roosters, where feathers fly in their quest to establish their maleness. Another game bird that struts its stuff is the spectacular looking great Argus pheasant (*Argusianus argus*). It is seldom seen but is often heard from a vantage point in jungle clearings in lowland and hill forests, where it parks itself to emit loud *kuang-kuang* hoots to attract females. The endemic Malay peacock pheasant (*Polyplectron malacense*) is a small, silent and sullen bird given to occasional bursts of noise, which sound more like angry explosive

RAJAH BROOKE'S BIRDWING BUTTERFLY

Male Rajah Brooke's birdwing (*Trogonoptera brookiana*) butterflies. Discovered by Alfred Russel Wallace in 1855, he named the species after James Brooke, the Rajah of Sarawak from 1841–68.

NOT TO SCALE

The atlas moth's (*Attacus atlas*) wings are patterned with triangle-shaped 'windows'.

shouts. In comparison, the crested wood partridge (*Rollulus rouloul*) is a devoted bird that values family life. It moves around in a group, foraging for insects and fruits on the floor of lowland and hill forests. The tiniest game bird in Malaysia is the cute 12.7 centimetre long blue-breasted quail (*Coturnix chinensis*), which lives in grassy areas.

Butterflies, moths and dragonflies are the other pretty damsels of the forest. These 'little' creatures of the rainforest make a big difference to the life and culture of the environment. Malaysia is home to a vast array of butterflies and moths including the celebrated Rajah Brooke's birdwing butterfly (*Trogonoptera brookiana*) and the atlas moth (*Attacus atlas*), the largest moth in the world. Butterflies are the glamour princesses of the rainforest—flitting from flower to flower, displaying their fancy appearance to best advantage in the light of day. Moths pale in comparison and prefer to come out in the darkness of the night.

Malaysia has over 1,000 butterfly species; the majority of species found in Peninsular Malaysia also occur in Sabah and Sarawak. There are more than 300 species of large-sized butterflies such as the birdwing and swallowtails (Papilionidae), whites and sulphurs (Pieridae), danaids, satyrids and amathusiids (Nymphalidae). Smaller butterflies are as beautiful and include the blues and hairstreaks (Lycaenidae) and skippers (Hesperiidae). More than 20 species are endemic to the Peninsula and are found in lowland forests, below an altitude of 750 metres. Some such as *Delia* butterflies are habitat-loyal, and are found only in forests at higher altitudes.

NEXT PAGE: Elephants move about in herds of 10–12, led by a few cows. Adult males usually lead a solitary life.

Malaysia is home to over 1,000 butterfly species, with a wide variety of forms, shapes and colours.

There are even more moths than butterflies in the rainforest; there are about 4,000 to 5,000 species of bigger macromoths and 6,000 species of smaller micromoths. Most are found in between lowland and montane forests, in the 500–1,000 metres above sea level zone. Endemics are common on Mount Kinabalu, with the *Diarsia barlowi* and *Phthonoloba titanis* occurring near the summit. For all their fragility, moths (and butterflies, too) are Ice Age survivors. These unique Mount Kinabalu summit moths are believed to have evolved from their ancestors who once inhabited the Himalayas during the Pleistocene global freezing. Indeed, fossil evidence discovered in France from 100 million years ago shows that butterflies and moths have strong survival skills, given their ability to metamorphose so as to protect themselves from predators. This intrinsic ability is seen in several butterflies and moths that engage in biological warfare—they release poison to kill the enemy. Those not privileged with these inbuilt systems resort to mimicry to repel attackers. The forewing of the atlas moth, for example, can be mistaken for the head of a snake. Caterpillars of the geometrid leaf-feeder (*Hyposidra talaca*) can pass off as a twig.

The other delicate jungle beauty, the dragonfly, is also made of stern stuff. Fossil evidence dating back 300 million years shows that the dragonfly was among the largest

The distinctive features of *Idea lynceus* sp. make it an easy species to identify.

The carnivorous damselfly (left and right) and dragonfly (centre) spend their early life in water—from the egg stage to nymph stage—only to fly off to land as winged adults.

insects to have ever existed, with a length of up to 30 centimetres and a 75-centimetre wingspan. Remarkably, they have not changed their form over time; they have just shrunk in size and now have a wingspan of about 20 centimetres. They live both on land and in water and are valuable, both aesthetically and scientifically. They are found perched on grasses growing in lakes and other water bodies but they are far from being mere decorative creatures. The adults prey on insect pests in paddy fields while their nymphs devour mosquito larvae, and are used as biological agents to control the mosquito population in water containers that are potentially mosquito-breeding grounds. Dragonflies are also indicators of the quality of freshwater; the more numerous, the better the water environment.

Malaysia's numerous rainforest habitats are also home to large populations of less attractive, frequently feared cold-blooded reptiles, which nonetheless add splashes of colour, while contributing to the bewildering diversity of the rainforest. They take on many shapes and forms, from harmless lizards to slithery snakes and crocodiles. Lizards are abundant in both rural and urban areas. In contrast, poisonous snakes are a rarity—there are only 17 poisonous land snakes compared to 144 species of non-poisonous ones. Most notorious are deadly pit vipers, which, unfortunately, occur near residential areas around paddy fields and rubber plantations. Most are arboreal and active both day and night, when they forage on rats and birds. But they are respected, even revered, and kept as symbols of good luck at the Penang Snake Temple, where the poisonous Wagler's pit viper (*Tropidolaemus wagleri*) is the star attraction.

The legendary six-metre long king cobra (*Ophiophagus hannah*) is another snake that engenders admiration in folk culture. It is the largest venomous snake in the world, but it is the venom of the more common black cobra (*Naja sumatranus*), which lurks around houses on forest fringes, that is more potent—it can kill the

The horned toad (*Megophrys* sp.) is also known as the rain toad because it croaks to announce the onset of rain.

victim in one to six hours, if not treated. Cobra meat is much sought after for its medicinal properties. It is also believed to be an aphrodisiac and a cobra gall bladder-and-wine concoction is said to cleanse the blood and improve the complexion.

Then, there are the 165 species of frogs and toads that live mainly in damp habitats. Hundreds of spiders, scorpions, millipedes, leeches and earthworms, bees, beetles, weevils, cicadas and an endless list of other insects and microorganisms live side-by-side, contributing to the rainforest eco-system. In turn the rainforest provides them with food, shelter and protection. Most have short life spans, but what they lack in longevity, they make up by their sheer numbers. Much maligned and viewed distastefully by man, they are really the little 'coolies' of the rainforest, working, mostly unseen, to collectively wield a powerful influence.

There are four species of porcupine found in Malaysia. The common porcupine (*Hystrix brachyura*) is found in both Peninsular and East Malaysia.

The rainforest is a dynamic environment, whirring away day and night like a lush green city that never sleeps. Its work is done quietly, often unnoticed, at all levels. Surfaces and strands of this mad muddle of towering, grasping, clinging, strangling and lowly plants are tightly woven together in a complex and intricate web of habitats and ecosystems. Nowhere else is the interdependence of living organisms more elaborately illustrated than in the species-rich tropical rainforest, which teems with millions of life forms ranging from microscopic bacteria to fungi, fruit bats, birds, insects, lizards, tapirs and tigers acting out

The herbivorous giant millipede is a common forest dweller.

their respective roles as prey, predator, pest, pollinator and perpetuator of the species in the endless drama of life and death to maintain the stability of this closed system.

An imaginary walk through Malaysia's rainforest will help us appreciate the workings of the dark and brooding world of tropical rainforests, which conceal rather than reveal their wondrous ways. Look afar; listen closely in this landscape of camouflages, fleeting movements, shadows and odours. Dawn begins with the chorus of gibbons from the treetops, the rainforest's wake-up call, with noisy reminders coming from the raucous helmeted hornbill. Both are fruit eaters, who forage fruit trees and scatter the seeds in their role as dispersers. Gibbons swing from tree to tree, across vast areas of the forest, picking ripe fruit from forest trees and lianas, eating the sweet flesh and dispersing the seeds. Many plants hidden under the tangle of lianas owe their continued existence to the feeding habits of these noisy

LEFT: Malaysia has a great variety of beetles, many of them agricultural pests.

RIGHT: Caterpillars are fussy eaters—they will only feed on certain leaves; butterflies and moths thus select only these plants on which to lay their eggs.

The tawny leopard cat (*Prionailurus bengalensis*), which is found in the forest, plantations and gardens, is notorious as a chicken thief.

forest dwellers. With growing light, new life forms come into view. Beetles can be spotted busily rolling bits of gibbon droppings through leaf litter, carrying them back to feed their young in their underground homes. These insects are the garbage recyclers, clearing the forest floor of animal waste, much of which is returned to the topsoil, aerating and fertilizing it along the way. But beware of soft-bodied leeches (Oligochaeta), the masters of camouflage which is their only protection against predators. They are among the earliest residents of the Malaysian rainforest, having evolved with it for over 100 million years. These parasites lie in wait to feed on their favourite meal—blood, of which they absorb several times their own body weight. Their bite is relatively mild and they transmit no disease.

The bark of rainforest trees is a mosaic of miniature landscapes, harbouring tiny spiders, mites, ants and bugs, perfect meals for squirrels that scamper along the trunks and branches. Squirrels also feed on the nutritious inner bark, especially the

WEAVER ANTS AT WORK

NOT TO SCALE

1. Weaver ants (*Oecophylla smaragdina*) first reach out to the nearest leaves on a tree.

2. They then draw the leaves together.

3. They secure the leaves with silk thread, obtainable only from a larva, which acts as a shuttle and tube of glue.

4. The community consisting of queen, males and workers move into their nest, which is jealously guarded.

sap-bearing *rengas* (*Gluta wallichi*) and beetles, grubs and termites burrowed in the bark. Longhorn beetles maintain the longevity of their own species by drilling and boring through the bark of common trees on which they live. Trees infested with these beetles are also perfect breeding grounds for termites and fungi, a lethal combination which slowly kills the trees.

By midday, the trees are on a photosynthetic overdrive, working silently and furiously at capturing sunlight, absorbing carbon dioxide from the air and water and minerals from the soil while the forest is lulled to sleep by the drowsy buzz of colonies of cicadas high up in the rainforest canopy. Butterflies flit about, with the Dark Blue Jungle Glory butterfly (*Thaumantis klugius lucipor*) providing a dash of colour in the darkest parts of the forest. Almost all butterflies fly by day, as do some moths. Many species visit flowers to feed on nectar and are also attracted to salt licks, decaying fruit, carrion and excrement. Caterpillars of all butterflies, however, feed only on plant matter. The butterfly lays its eggs on a leaf surface of a food plant. The hatched caterpillar feeds on the plant tissue, moulting as it grows. After the final moult, the skin of the caterpillar hardens to form the case of the pupa, which is usually suspended by fine threads from a twig. After two to three weeks, the butterfly emerges. Within hours the wings expand and harden and it flies off, in search of a mate.

Small forest lizards can often be seen basking in patches of sunlight. Energized by the sun, they skitter through the dry leaves, usually pausing to prey on insects. The forest enters snooze-control in the afternoon,

An angry mob of *kerengga* (weaver ants) attack a grasshopper, which has intruded into their home ground.

THE FLYING SQUIRREL

The red-cheeked flying squirrel (*Hylopetes spadiceus*) enjoys the power of flight by spreading out the membrane of skin between its fore and hind limbs. It then glides smoothly and swiftly downwards from one tree to another in search of food or to escape predators.

NOT TO SCALE

A bee's nest hanging from the branch of a *tualang (Koompassia excelsa)* tree, a favoured nesting place for wild honey bees.

only to suddenly burst into activity with a bird party, when a motley contingent of leaf birds, nectar feeders and flycatchers progress through the forest, scouring for food at every level from canopy to the forest floor. At dusk, squadrons of ants begin their march out of their nests between the tree roots, from the fearsome but friendly giant forest ant (*Camponotus gigas*) to the nocturnal fire ant (*Solenopsis geminata*) that begin to swarm across the forest floor. Generally sociable, these insects are communal creatures that turn into vicious foes when disturbed; intrusions such as human feet are often repelled with a swift and stinging retaliation. An incredible average of 2,000 ants inhabits every square metre of soil in the Pasoh Forest Reserve in Peninsular Malaysia. They are the main predators of other insects in the lowlands but higher up the mantle is passed on to centipedes and millipedes. Other small rainforest predators are scorpions (Arachnida) and spiders (Araneae), both with poisonous stings. Bees, hornets and wasps (all Hymenoptera) also have painful stings but bees, especially, are useful as pollinators and for their honey, beeswax, royal jelly and bee pollen.

The serow (*Capricornis sumatraensis*) is a solitary animal that lives on limestone hills.

THE LONE WILD GOAT

Described as a large, goat-like animal with straight, unbranched horns, the serow (*Capricornis sumatraensis*) is the lone representative of wild goats in Malaysia. Locally, it is known as *kambing gurun* (desert goat) or *kambing hutan* (forest goat), two names which are indicative of its habitat: the steep forested slopes and desolate limestone outcrops in the north and central regions of Malaysia—not the most hospitable of environments.

The serow grows to about a metre in height at the shoulder, and is predominantly dark brown in colour with tinges of grey or red. It has a mane, is usually solitary, and because of its pre-ferred habitat, more agile than most hoofed animals.

Naturalists do not consider it a true goat, but concede that it is related to the European chamois and the North American Rocky Mountain goat, two animals that have built reputations on their agility in moving about with ease in mountainous areas and other difficult terrain.

Darkness falls quickly in the rainforest, and is announced by the wailing trumpet call of the six o'clock cicada that settles to a sleepy hum. The night choir begins with a chorus of crickets and small frogs. In the dark rainforest, you are likely to be startled by the glint, glitter or stares of luminous creatures of the night while swatting pesky mosquitoes seeking blood, especially in forests by the river or swamp. You may sense the presence of the white furry *tikus bulan* or moonrat (*Echinosorex gymnurus*) from its awful odour (supposedly the worst in the forest), as it shuffles about damp and dark crevices looking for earthworms. Another smelly denizen found in Sabah and Sarawak is the *teledu* (*Mydaus javanensis*), an otter that lives by the forest edge. Listen to the sounds of armies of termites and ants. See the sparkle of fireflies and patches of fluorescent fungi on fallen branches, twigs and leaves. Snails glide about, in search of plant matter, using their feelers to probe their way through the forest floor. Centipedes prey on insects while scorpions often lie in wait before burrows to pounce on their prey.

Listen out, too, for the hiss of slithery snakes, ranging from the pencil-size harmless variety to the reticulated python (*Python reticulatus*), which can grow up to four metres or more. With a flashlight you may succeed at observing some nocturnal wildlife. Larger mammals such as the civet, tapir, tiger, rhinoceros, deer, gaur, wild boar and serow are common enough in the rainforest but rarely seen, either day or night. With some luck, the big-eyed slow loris may come within view, skulking across the branches before pouncing on its prey, mainly insects and frogs. Or you may have a close encounter with the incredibly shy mouse deer, rarely seen by day but it can come up close and personal in the beam of the flashlight.

'Bagai kelip-kelip terbang malam.'
Like a firefly flying by night.

MALAY PROVERB REFERRING TO
A SUPPOSED SECRET WHICH
IS WIDELY KNOWN.

CHAPTER FIVE

PEOPLE OF THE RAINFOREST

Peninsular Malaysia's rainforest is home to 18 aboriginal tribes, known collectively as the Orang Asli (original people). According to some sources, Anthony Ratos, whose attachment to the simple, fascinating people of the Malaysian jungle began at the tender age of 12, coined the term 'Orang Asli' in 1952, in a thesis on the aborigines he submitted when he was a trainee teacher at Kirkby Teachers College in Liverpool, United Kingdom. The phrase gained popular currency and is now used as the generic term for all indigenous tribes living in Peninsular Malaysia. Ratos, who later worked as deputy director of the Department of Orang Asli Affairs in Pahang, has built a strong reputation for promoting aboriginal culture over the years.

In 2000, there were approximately 116,000 Orang Asli representing 0.5 per cent of the national population. They are, however, not a homogeneous group, with each tribe maintaining their own language, culture and way of life. Officially, they have been divided into three main groups: the Negritos, the Senoi and the Proto-Malays, with each group consisting of six tribes. The Kensiu, Kintak, Jahai, Lanoh, Mendriq and Bateq are known as the Negritos, the oldest inhabitants of Peninsular Malaysia. They arrived here some 25,000 years ago. Sometimes referred to as the purest race in the country, they are of short stature with frizzy hair and dark skin. Resembling the tribes of Papua New Guinea, they are thought to belong to the Paleo-Melanesian race that originated in mainland Southeast Asia and passed through the region on their way to present-day Melanesia. The Senoi came next, following the same route. They consist of the Semai, Temiar, Semaq Beri, Che' Wong, Jah Hut and the Mah Meri, who together form the largest Orang Asli group in the Peninsula. Both the Negrito and Senoi languages—now called Aslian—sound like the Austro-Asiatic languages of the indigenous peoples of Myanmar, Thailand, Cambodia and Vietnam. The Temuan, Semelai, Jakun, Orang Kanak, Orang Kuala and Orang Seletar, known as Proto-Malays, on the other hand, arrived last on the Peninsula and trace their origins back to the Indonesian islands; their languages are somewhat similar to Malay, which belongs to the Austronesian family of languages.

A traditional bird trap made from a coconut shell.

OPPOSITE: Tama Usong, a Kayan chief, c. 1900. Traditionally farmers, the Kayans dominate the Baram and Rejang river basins of Central Borneo.

Children of the Jahai tribe, found mainly in the remote jungles of northeast Peninsular Malaysia. The Jahai belong to the Negrito group of Orang Asli, the oldest aboriginal group in Malaysia.

Source: Department of Orang Asli Affairs (JHEOA) 2000

TABLE 1

ORANG ASLI POPULATION IN PENINSULAR MALAYSIA

NEGRITOS	
Kensiu	254
Kintak	150
Jahai	1,244
Lanoh	173
Mendriq	167
Bateq	1,519
SENOI	
Che' Wong	234
Jah Hut	2,594
Mah Meri	3,503
Semai	34,248
Semaq Beri	2,348
Temiar	17,706
PROTO-MALAYS	
Jakun	21,484
Orang Kanak	73
Orang Kuala	3,221
Orang Seletar	1,037
Semelai	5,026
Temuan	18,560
OTHERS	2,578
TOTAL	**116,119**

With successive waves of migration, first by the Malays, and followed much later by the Chinese and the Indians, the Orang Asli found themselves being moved either to the coast or further into the forested highlands. Today, about 40 per cent of them live close to or within forested areas, with the rest concentrated along the coast. The Negritos, the smallest and most isolated of them all, are found mainly in the northern and eastern parts of the Peninsula, where they follow a semi-nomadic lifestyle along the foothills of the Main Range that forms the spine of the peninsula. According to 2000 figures, there are only 3,507 of these shy and peaceful people in the Peninsula, constituting less than three per cent of the Orang Asli population (*see Table 1*). As the oldest forest dwellers in Malaysia, Negritos have the distinction of having forged strong links with their rainforest home. Indeed, they have a reputation for identifying rainforest plants better than many botanists do and recognizing animal tracks and sounds more accurately than most zoologists. Given their long relationship with the forest, it is not surprising that they are experts on the uses of all manner of forest plants and produce.

The largest Orang Asli group in the Peninsula is the Senoi, with 60,633 accounting for just over half the total Orang Asli population. They are found mainly in the central mountain range and its foothills, where they have led a more settled lifestyle for several centuries. They engage in hill rice cultivation and trade in jungle products such as durian, *petai*, rattan and resins with the Malay communities living on the forest fringes.

Proto-Malays, with a current population of 49,401 were the last group of aborigines to arrive in the Peninsula. They settled mainly along the coast, as fishermen, and although they lived in relative isolation from other communities, there were some economic dealings and social interaction between the Orang Asli and neighbouring Malay communities dating back to as far back as the 5th century AD. Proto-Malays living in remote forests exchanged jungle products for salt, knives and metal axe heads with Malay villagers. An early 19th-century report tells of Negritos presenting forest products to the Malay chiefs who controlled the river basins where they lived.

It was only in 1953 that there was a coordinated effort by the colonial government of the day to integrate the Orang Asli into mainstream Malaya. The Department of Aborigines, later renamed Jabatan Hal Ehwal Orang Asli (JHEOA) (Department of Orang Asli Affairs) was established to look after their welfare. The Orang Asli were introduced to education, health and consumer goods through the establishment of schools, medical dispensaries and trading stores staffed by the department's personnel. Since then, Orang Asli

BLOWING AWAY THE GAME

Making a blowpipe is one of the few true specialties among the rainforest dwellers of Malaysia and it takes a blowpipe specialist one day to make a complete set. A dozen or so different plants are used to make the precision tool. The main body parts, quivers and inserts are made from several species of bamboo; the mouthpiece is shaped from resinous damar, found hardened on the bark of dipterocarp trees. The *Arenga* palm is another raw material—its bark is used to join the bamboo barrel parts; its leaves are split to make darts; and the lightweight pith forms the cone of the dart. When ready for use, the cone is coated with poison obtained from the sap of the ipoh tree (*Antiaris toxicaria*). The hunter carries this lethal preparation in a stoppered bamboo tube. In the hands of a master blowpiper, this traditional hunting tool is an accurate shot on small game within 20 metres.

A Jakun hunter on the quiet waters of Tasik Cini, Pahang.

communities have been integrated gradually into mainstream society. Even the nomadic Negritos, who were once exclusively hunters and gatherers, have been known to settle down to more conventional living arrangements in government land schemes developed by agencies such as the Federal Land Development Authority (FELDA), where they cultivate agricultural crops. But their rainforest ways are not all lost; every so often they return to the forest to gather products such as rattan, bamboo and medicinal plants.

Some are oblivious to the changes occurring around them and pursue a more semi-nomadic lifestyle. The Senoi Temiar tribe, for example, prefers to be hill rice growers in the highlands. The cooler climate is more conducive for hard, physical labour in the outdoors; water-borne and mosquito-borne diseases are rare in settlements around rushing hillside streams; and fewer pests infest their rice and crops cultivated on the slopes. The extremely shy Bateq are a semi-nomadic Negrito tribe who range the mighty rainforest of Taman Negara National Park.

An Orang Asli woman harvesting bamboo shoots, a local delicacy.

LEFT AND MIDDLE: Basket-weaving is a common craft amongst aboriginal tribes.

RIGHT: *Petai*, a popular Malay salad vegetable, is harvested for both home use and for sale in nearby villages.

A Bateq pulls his child and bamboo raft through the rapids of Lata Berkoh waterfall in Taman Negara, Pahang.

They are mainly hunters and gatherers; the men hunt small game such as wild pigs and monkeys with spears and blowpipes while the women gather fruits and roots such as tubers from the climbing plants of the genus *Dioscorea*, a rich source of carbohydrates. A few Bateq have become national park guides, while the women are known for handicraft such as bamboo combs and hair clips, which are sold as souvenirs at Taman Negara National Park.

A similar lifestyle is observed among the Jakun living in Pahang on the shores of Tasik Cini, Malaysia's largest natural lake after Tasik Bera (*see p33*). They have lived there for centuries, fishing the lake for food. A folk tale tells of a magical dragon that lives in the water, guarding an ancient city of gold that once occupied an island in the middle of the lake. This legend and their sound knowledge of the area make this community of Orang Asli fascinating guides to Tasik Cini, a popular tourist attraction. Like the Bateq women, Jakun women often supplement their income by selling handicraft as souvenirs.

Orang Asli such as the Temuans, who live in aboriginal settlements closer to towns and cities, have adopted semi-urban lifestyles. Many are employed in nearby towns. Government agencies such as the Federal Land Consolidation and

MATERIALS FROM THE FOREST

NOT TO SCALE

Mengkuang

Bamboo

Chengal tree

Bertam

Rattan

Rehabilitation Authority (FELCRA) advised them on oil palm cultivation. They also introduced them to hydroponics, a water-based food cultivation practice.

While little is known of the Orang Asli of Peninsular Malaysia internationally, tales of the indigenous people of Borneo, with headhunters, bare-breasted tattooed women, *orang pendek* (short men), men with tails and other exotica, have fascinated the world over since the 1800s. Much of this now belongs to the realms of history or fiction.

The indigenous tribes of Sarawak (*see Table 2, p130*) number as many as 37 known groups and sub-groups. The Ibans or Dayaks (once referred to as the Sea Dayaks) are the most populous group, constituting 30 per cent of the state's population in 2000. The Bidayuh or Land Dayaks make up another eight per cent. Other indigenous tribes collectively known as Orang Ulu (upriver people) are the people of the interior. As with the Orang Asli, each group has its own culture and language.

It is difficult to categorize and conclusively specify their numbers but it is estimated that there are 39 different ethnic groups in Sabah. Most numerous are the Kadazan Dusuns making up 24 per cent of the state's population in 2000, followed by the Bajau at 17 per cent (*see Table 3, p130*).

Physically, the indigenous tribes of Sabah and Sarawak resemble the Malays with their South Chinese features: medium stature, yellowish brown or brown skin, straight, dark hair and wide, flat faces. Their languages belong to the Austronesian family of languages that traces its origins to Vietnam and Cambodia to the north, Madagascar to the west and Micronesia, Melanesia and Polynesia to the east.

NEXT PAGE: Good hunting dogs are prized items among the nomadic tribes, who take their animals along on food-gathering trips across land and water.

Jungle homes are often simple lean-to affairs with roofs made from the fronds of the *bertam* palm (*Eugeissona tristis*).

A Kenyah tribe in Long Sibatu, c.1900. Kenyahs are mainly farmers found as close neighbours of the Kayans in the interior of Sarawak. These tribes are classified as Orang Ulu, or 'upriver people.'

Source: Department of Statistics (Sarawak) 2000

TABLE 2

SARAWAK POPULATION BY ETHNIC GROUP

Bidayuh	166,756
Chinese	537,230
Iban	603,735
Malay	462,270
Melanau	112,984
Other Indigenous	117,690
Others	8,103
TOTAL	**2,008,768**

TABLE 3

Source: Department of Statistics (Sabah) 2000

SABAH POPULATION BY ETHNIC GROUP

Bajau	343,178
Chinese	262,115
Kadazan Dusun	479,944
Malay	303,497
Murut	84,679
Other Indigenous	390,058
Others	125,190
TOTAL	**1,988,661**

Even though there is evidence of human habitation in the Niah Caves some 35,000–40,000 years ago, the Austronesian ancestors of the indigenous peoples of Borneo left China to settle here only about 4,500 years ago, mainly as hunters and gatherers.

Three key developments that occurred over the past 2,000 years in Borneo possibly explain for the dramatic differences between the indigenous people on this island and the Orang Asli of Peninsular Malaysia. First, the arrival of Indian and Chinese traders in Borneo since the first century AD resulted in increased contacts between the indigenous tribes and the outside world. This meant that they were exposed to trade and other factors, which may have caused them to abandon a nomadic lifestyle for a more sedentary one.

Second, the use and manufacture of metal implements led to shifting cultivation and other settled agriculture. Third, the decisive penetration of the interior initially by British colonialists and later, the federal government, for cultivation of cash crops such as sago and pepper, mining, forestry and oil extraction led to large-scale migration across major parts of the interior. Occurring at different times and intensities, these factors have resulted in the gradual integration of indigenous communities into the mainstream culture of Malaysia.

However, despite prolonged exposure to the outside world, many Sabah and Sarawak ethnic groups still retain their deep respect for and dependence on the rainforest till this day. A clear pattern can be discerned, reflecting the different levels of integration among the many tribes. Generally, the forest nomads in the interior tend to act as suppliers of jungle products to the more settled agriculturists, who are both end users and middlemen in a trading chain that links the people of the interior to the Chinese, Malay and other urban communities along the coast. The Orang Ulu of Sarawak are mainly forest nomads living in simple lean-tos of saplings, palm leaves and tree bark; some build huts either on the ground or on stilts. Nomadic bands vary from 30–40 people up to 150–200, who either move within the same area or migrate over long distances, usually overland. Largely self-sufficient, they hunt and gather for two

Tama Bulan, a Kenyah chief, c. 1900.

THE LONGHOUSE

Longhouse living is exclusive to the people of Borneo. A longhouse is really a village, with all the villagers living under a common roof. It can be likened to a row of terraces, with each home or compartment separated by walls and sharing a common street. Except, the entire structure—home and road—are several feet above the ground. Longhouse dwellers are not necessarily related; often they are independent members of the same tribe.

Each family has its own home or compartment, with sleeping and cooking areas. The cooking areas are considered the 'female' part of the house and are off-limits to outsiders, especially men. Here the 'lady of the house' cooks and cleans, as well as socializes with the other women. Adjoining the row of compartments is a common covered corridor or *ruai*, the men's domain. Here, guests are entertained, public meetings held and major rituals performed. Men also gather in the *ruai* for daily chores such as mending fishnets and traps.

It is assumed that this style of housing developed as a defensive measure to protect the village from tribal attacks especially in the old head-hunting days. It was easier to protect the village when it was gathered in one common structure. Longhouses are difficult to access, especially since the ladders are withdrawn at night as a security measure. Some longhouses

The longhouse is unique to Borneo, where the entire village community is often housed in one raised block of terraces with a common porch.

were also fortified with earthworks, trenches and palisades around them.

The raised structure also protects the longhouse from the effects of floods and the ground level is used as a storehouse and shelter for animals. In addition, the use of natural materials such as bamboo and timber results in a cool well-ventilated area—combatting the sweltering heat and humidity of the tropics.

Variations in longhouse design occur between the ethnic groups. Iban villages

usually have only one longhouse each, generally built of lightwood and bamboo. Kenyah and Maloh villages, on the other hand, consist of several longhouses, usually massive structures built on heavy hardwood posts with timber flooring high above the ground. House decorations are used to denote rank. The walls, doors, rafters and adjacent *ruai* posts belonging to important chiefs are often carved with elaborate motifs; the more elaborate, the higher up in the longhouse hierarchy he is.

reasons—for themselves and for trade. Their staple food is sago (*Metroxylon sagu*) which they obtain by felling sago palms in the coastal swamplands. Further inland they harvest another sago species (*Eugeissona utilis*). This is supplemented with fruits such as durian, rambutan and mangosteen; vegetables and fern leaves. They are also skilled hunters, capturing gibbons, macaques, civets, squirrels, reptiles and birds with blowpipes; larger animals such as wild boar and deer are hunted on foot with spear and dog.

From time immemorial, a whole range of rainforest products were collected for sale; first to traders from China and India and later to settlers along the coast. Aromatic woods like *gaharu* bark (*Aquilaria* sp.) were sought for incense and *ketapang* fruit (*Terminalia catappa*) for dyeing and tanning. Latex from trees such as *gutta percha* (*Palaquium* spp.) was used for insulating telegraph wires. Resin from *damar minyak* (*Agathis borneensis*) was used for sealing. Rattan was used for binding. Vegetable tallow was made from the seeds of the illipe nut (*Shorea* sp.).

Animal products, too, had a ready market. Prized items were the saliva-impregnated nests of the swiftlet (*Collocalia fuciphaga* and *C. maxima*), a Chinese delicacy, as well as the bezoar stones (stones found inside animal bodies) of the long-tailed monkey (*Presbytis hosei* and *P. rubicunda*). Other high-demand items were pangolin (*Manis javanica*) scales for magical charms, the feathers of the rhinoceros hornbill (*Buceros rhinoceros*) and great argus pheasant (*Argusianus argus*) to decorate the tribal headdress of many of the indigenous folk of Sabah and Sarawak. The hardened casque of the helmeted hornbill (*Buceros vigil*) was sought to fashion carvings and jewellery.

BASKETWARE PATTERNS

Sarawak basketware weavers very often base their patterns on fauna and flora. Various combinations of different materials and colours create subtle effects.

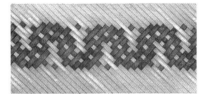

1. Creeper

2. Bamboo shoots

3. Leeches

4. Durian flowers

5. Birds

FROM HEAD-HUNTERS TO MILITARY MEN

Sarawak's Ibans, once head-hunters, have an illustrious record as fine military men. Iban fighting is different from that of other Borneans. They put a premium on open displays of bravery and full frontal attacks. It is this sort of fearlessness that has earned them the privilege of being recruited to form the crack military outfit called the Sarawak Rangers.

The Sarawak Rangers played a pivotal role in fighting against the Japanese during the Japanese Occupation (1941–45), against the communists during the Malayan Emergency (1948–60) and the Indonesians during their conflict with Malaysia (1963–65). Their name inspires admiration among the ranks of the population and Malaysia's armed forces in particular.

Trophies of war, skulls hanging from the rafters of a Kayan longhouse, c. 1900.

TYPICAL PHASES IN SHIFTING CULTIVATION

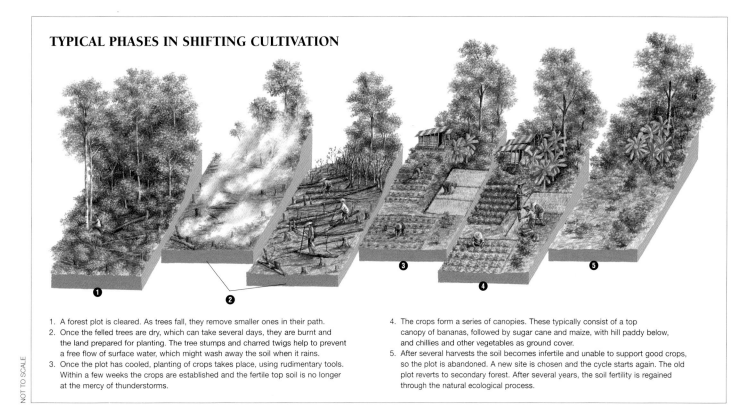

1. A forest plot is cleared. As trees fall, they remove smaller ones in their path.
2. Once the felled trees are dry, which can take several days, they are burnt and the land prepared for planting. The tree stumps and charred twigs help to prevent a free flow of surface water, which might wash away the soil when it rains.
3. Once the plot has cooled, planting of crops takes place, using rudimentary tools. Within a few weeks the crops are established and the fertile top soil is no longer at the mercy of thunderstorms.
4. The crops form a series of canopies. These typically consist of a top canopy of bananas, followed by sugar cane and maize, with hill paddy below, and chillies and other vegetables as ground cover.
5. After several harvests the soil becomes infertile and unable to support good crops, so the plot is abandoned. A new site is chosen and the cycle starts again. The old plot reverts to secondary forest. After several years, the soil fertility is regained through the natural ecological process.

NOT TO SCALE

Scattered across the rainforest are longhouses occupied by the more settled farmers. They practise shifting cultivation, with rice as the main crop intermixed with a variety of other crops such as cucumber, gourd, mustard greens, beans, pumpkin, pepper, chilli, maize and taro. Fruits such as banana, pineapple and papaya are also grown. Sugar cane is usually planted along with other crops such as tapioca on small patches following the harvest. This ecologically friendly farming practice utilizes a range of available microenvironments and nutrients. It also minimizes risks because there is no over-dependence on a limited number of food sources.

The rainforest dwellers of Malaysia are animists, who believe that everything, both animate and inanimate, has a spirit that mirrors the events in their lives. Benevolent spirits will bless good deeds, rewarded usually with bountiful harvests and a blessed life. Misdemeanours, on the other hand, will unleash a volley of malevolent spirits that will wreak havoc on the person, the family, and even the community. An ambivalent attitude towards the spirit world exists. Forest spirits are respected and revered because of their perceived ability to bestow believers with food, raw materials and other comforts of life; but the forest can also be a dangerous place, where evil lurks in the form of wild animals preying on the innocent. Man-eating tigers and stampeding elephants are common occurrences in their home environment.

These beautifully carved bamboo tobacco containers exhibit foliage motifs taken from nature.

NEXT PAGE: Planting rice in Bario, Sarawak. The placation of 'rice spirits' is important to ensure a bountiful rice crop.

Jah Hut and Mah Meri woodcarvings are sought-after by art galleries and museums around the world.

This spiritual ambivalence is clearly seen among the Mah Meri of Carey Island, Selangor, who subscribe to two diametrically opposed views in their relationship with the environment. They justify their consumption of plants and animals, which are believed to have been *tulah* (cursed) and therefore condemned to serve as food for human beings. On the other hand, they believe that the destruction of the environment is *kemali* (taboo) and wrongdoers will be punished with bad luck, or worse, death!

Among these predominantly agrarian communities, the rice spirit emerges as the most powerful in the pantheon of deities. Rice has since time immemorial been the focal point of both the economic and religious life of the indigenous tribes of Malaysia. They believe the rice spirits gave the knowledge of rice and its cultivation to humans; therefore the rice spirits must be appeased at all costs, taking rice cultivation rituals to elaborate heights. The growing season begins with supplications to the guardian spirits of the soil before clearing the land, with every subsequent stage marked by rituals appealing to benign spirits to protect the crop from the evil spirits that can cause disease and other damage. Except for

Jah Hut woodcarvings of animal spirits.

CARVING OUT A FINE TRADITION

Woodcarvings, especially those by the Jah Hut of Pahang and the Mah Meri of Carey Island, are included in the collections of art galleries and museums, both in Malaysia and overseas. Although the communities live far apart—the Mah Meri are a coastal people living 40 kilometres from Kuala Lumpur, while the Jah Hut live in the jungles of Jerantut, Pahang—they are united in their passion for wood sculpture.

The Mah Meri and Jah Hut belong to the Senoi racial group and are animists; their woodcarvings are an artistic expression of their world of spirits. Each piece has a story behind it, usually a mythological tale recounted by the medicine man or shaman. The stories help the people understand the secrets of life and nature and are also a part of their rich oral tradition.

As a sea-based society, Mah Meri carvings often depict the spirits of the water. Popular subjects among them are the *moyang belangkas* (horseshoe crab spirit) and *moyang katak kala* (frog spirit). Jah Hut sculptures, meanwhile, dwell on jungle spirits such as the *bes gajah* (elephant spirit), *bes makan* (handeating spirit) and *bes jin tanah* (spirit of the soil). These Orang Asli carvers have produced an impressive body of work. Their sculptures reflect a natural understanding of the formal elements of sculpting, where space, line, form and shape meld into spontaneous and harmonious pieces of art.

Above and below: A Mah Meri woodcarver uses only simple tools to demonstrate his carving skills at an exhibition of Orang Asli art held at the Kuala Lumpur Craft Complex.

BASKETWARE FROM SABAH AND SARAWAK

Sabah and Sarawak's rich weave-craft tradition has spawned a cottage industry that produces a variety of baskets, mats and decorative items.

Tanam lalang tak akan tumbuh padi.
'If you plant weeds you won't get padi.'

MALAY PROVERB

A vanishing practice, pounding rice by hand; rice flour is the main ingredient in many local dishes.

normal tasks involving reaping, threshing and storing, rice must not be struck, abused or discarded. If, by chance, the rice spirit is displeased by disrespectful behaviour, a ritual of apology has to be performed.

The highlight of the annual indigenous calendar is the harvest festival known as *gawai padi* in Sarawak and *tadau ka'amatan* in Sabah (or Kadazan Harvest Festival). This festival is based on the belief that 'without rice, there is no life' and is the culmination of a series of offerings made to the rice spirit from the sowing of the first seed. The festival is a celebration to thank the rice spirits who have blessed the community with a good harvest. The main ritual involves shamans and priestesses performing ceremonial dances to thank the rice spirits and at the same time supplicating for a year of plenty ahead.

RAINFOREST MUSIC FESTIVAL

The annual Rainforest Music Festival held every July in Kuching, Sarawak, is a celebration of the rich song and dance heritage of indigenous people from all over the world. Performers from Mongolia to Madagascar and Sudan to Scotland converge at the Sarawak Cultural Village for the three-day festival, which revolves around concerts, dance performances, folk songs, workshops and story-telling sessions. The festival is also a platform for the promotion of the indigenous culture of Sarawak. The festival highlight centres on the tribal music of drums, flutes, zithers and *sape* (lute) that are part and parcel of the cultural heritage of the indigenous communities such as the Bisayah, Bidayuh and Iban and the Orang Ulu of Sarawak.

Sarawak's Rainforest Music Festival, which promotes indigenous music, has a growing following from around the world.

OPPOSITE: Metal accessories form part of the ceremonial dress of Iban men and women. The women are best-known for the *rawai*, a corset of rattan hoops secured by small brass rings and stiffened at intervals with metal wires.

Animistic rituals have long been the mainstay of indigenous cultural life. But times are changing for many communities, who have changed old ways for new. Many have embraced Islam and Christianity and abandoned animistic practices. National economic development programmes have made their impact, transforming the lives of many forest communities. More and more are adapting to a sedentary lifestyle, and some traditions are being eroded with increasing exposure not only to mainstream Malaysia but also the rest of the globalized world. Head-hunting and bare-breasted women belong to the annals of history while body tattooing, textile weaving, beadwork and other indigenous crafts are on the wane. Traditional attire such as the headdress, loincloth, *rawai* (rattan corsets) and silver jewellery are now reserved for ceremonial functions, with Western attire and the Malay *baju* adopted as the choice of dress for daily use. Efforts have been made to arrest the loss of their rich cultural traditions. But change is inevitable as the rainforest dwellers of Malaysia catch up with the times as citizens of the nation.

An Iban carved wooden mask used to scare naughty children with its staring, wide eyes and prominent teeth and lips.

CHAPTER SIX

PRODUCTS OF THE FOREST

M alaysia is one of the world's largest producers of tropical timbers and timber products, thanks to its vast reserves of natural rainforest. The timber sector, one of the country's traditional sources of revenue, is a major player in the national economy, generating 4.5 per cent of the country's Gross Domestic Product and employing more than a quarter million people. In 2001, Malaysian timber and timber exports earned RM14.3 billion (USD3.8 billion).

The Malaysian timber industry has had a long and, sometimes, bumpy ride. It began in Sabah in the 1900s, when logging was the mainstay of the economy of British North Borneo, the colonial name for Sabah. In 1941 Sabah ranked as the third largest exporter of timber in the British Empire and the town of Sandakan was one of the leading timber ports of the world. Timber became a major export item in the 1920s and 1930s in Sarawak. The industry made a relatively late entry to Peninsular Malaysia in 1945. By the 1960s and early 1970s, Malaysia had become a formidable force in the international trade of tropical hardwoods, which after rubber and palm oil, ranked as the third most important revenue earner for the country.

The industry came under attack in the late 1980s when environmentalists declared war on tropical timber and branded logging the scourge of rainforests. Waving the 'Save the Rainforests' banner, they called for a boycott of tropical timber based on the argument that logging caused irreparable damage to the global environment, citing global warming and ozone depletion as examples. Tropical forestry was portrayed as the bogeyman, causing havoc on Planet Earth. Hard-line tactics were used to drive home this message. 'Green' activists even waylaid tropical timber-laden ships at destination ports, causing immeasurable embarrassment and bad press. Exports to European and American markets were affected.

To provide for a coordinated approach to forestry, the National Forestry Council (NFC), comprising the chief ministers of the 13 Malaysian states and chaired by the Deputy Prime Minister, was established in 1971. This council provides a forum for policy formulation and to address problems and issues relating to forestry administration and management. To provide for good forest management practices,

Bamboo containers used to store live fish while fishing in paddy fields.

OPPOSITE: A finely carved *chempaka* timber panel at Malaysian Timber Council headquarters in Kuala Lumpur.

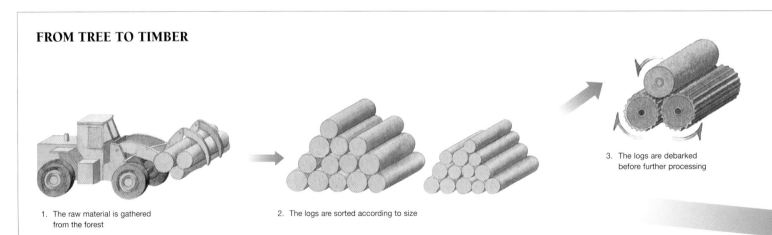

In Malaysia, timber is removed from the forest by trucks that use designated logging trails; an integral part of reduced impact logging (RIL) practices associated with sustainable forestry.

the National Forestry Policy was formulated in 1978. This was followed by the enactment of the National Forestry Act in 1984. To further strengthen its provisions to safeguard and protect the forest resources from illegal logging, the Act was amended in 1993. The country's commitment ensures that at least 50 per cent of the country's land mass will remain permanently under forest cover. Meanwhile, agencies such as the Forest Research Institute Malaysia (FRIM) and other research institutions were asked to develop technology that would maximize wood usage, minimize waste and upgrade environmental controls. After its formation in 1992, the Malaysian Timber Council (MTC), assumed a more frontline role; among other functions, it was tasked with disseminating information on Malaysia's forest management practices and its timber industry in the international arena.

The national industrialization policy called for more downstream processing of Malaysian timber at home, spurring the growth of a variety of wood-based industries. This has helped shape the Malaysian timber industry in the late 1980s and 1990s. Log production fell from 40 million m^3 in 1990 to 23.1 million m^3 in 2000. This reduction is partly attributed to the move towards sustainable forest management practices. There is also a decline in the conversion of natural forests

FROM TREE TO TIMBER

1. The raw material is gathered from the forest

2. The logs are sorted according to size

3. The logs are debarked before further processing

Before plywood (veneer) and sawntimber are produced, the base material is sorted and prepared for further processing.

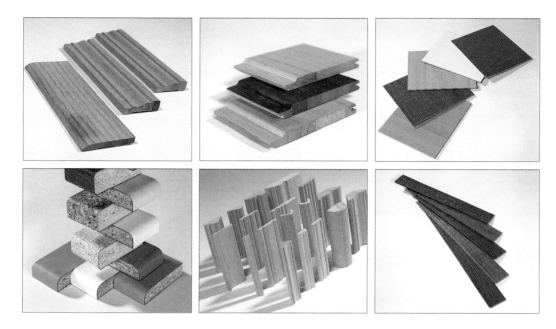

A selection of Malaysian timber products.

for agriculture and industrial uses. To reduce pressure on natural forests, forest plantation development is encouraged in order to supplement the raw material timber requirements of the country. Meanwhile, the export profile has undergone dramatic changes in the last 20 years. Once logs reigned supreme as primary revenue earners; but in the current landscape, several other products have usurped their position, including sawntimber, panel products such as plywood, medium density fibreboard (MDF), particleboard, chipboard, mouldings, builders' carpentry and joinery (BCJ) and furniture.

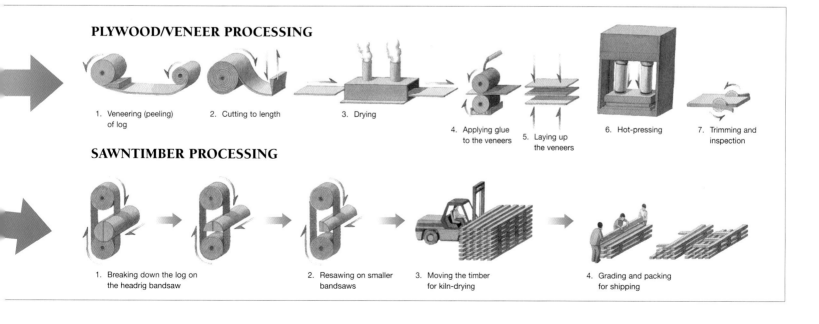

PLYWOOD/VENEER PROCESSING

1. Veneering (peeling) of log
2. Cutting to length
3. Drying
4. Applying glue to the veneers
5. Laying up the veneers
6. Hot-pressing
7. Trimming and inspection

SAWNTIMBER PROCESSING

1. Breaking down the log on the headrig bandsaw
2. Resawing on smaller bandsaws
3. Moving the timber for kiln-drying
4. Grading and packing for shipping

A well-designed kitchen cabinet made from Malaysian rubberwood.

OPPOSITE: Fine local woods are often used in hotel and office lobbies in a tribute to the rich timber-based architectural heritage of the country.

Turning wood for furniture components; Malaysia has a buoyant furniture industry.

Sawntimber, a primary raw material used for construction, mouldings, joinery and furniture, is derived from hardwoods from dipterocarp species such as *meranti* (*Shorea* spp.), *keruing* (*Dipterocarpus* spp.), *resak* (*Cotylelobium* spp. and *Vatica* spp.), *chengal* (*Neobalanocarpus heimii*), *mersawa* (*Anisoptera* spp.), *balau* (*Shorea* spp.) and *kapur* (*Dryobalanops* spp.). While almost half of it is used by domestic wood-processing and construction industries, sawntimber is still a major contributor of export ringgit. In 2001, it earned a substantial RM2.17 billion (USD571 million), with exports mainly to The Netherlands, Japan and Thailand. Used mainly in the building industry, plywood products also have a somewhat similar pattern. Combined exports of plywood, blockboard and panels such as MDF and particleboard recorded total sales of RM4.5 billion (USD1.2 billion) in 2001. Preferred species for plywood and blockboard are a mixture of mixed medium hardwoods and mixed light hardwoods which include red, yellow and white *meranti*, *mersawa*, *keruing* and *nyatoh* (spp. of Sapotaceae).

While research and development (R&D) efforts have started to pay off, organizations such as the Malaysian Timber Industry Board (MTIB) and MTC have spearheaded efforts to position Malaysia as a world leader in tropical timbers and timber products against the backdrop of stiff competition and trade liberalization. In the international market, the biggest gains have been achieved by the furniture industry. It has been extremely vibrant since the 1990s, having surpassed industry and government expectations. In 1980, wooden and rattan furniture earned a modest RM269.5 million (USD130.5 million). In 2001, the figure had swelled to RM3.8 billion (USD1 billion), after having recorded an annual growth rate of 30–40 per cent in the last decade.

In the development of the Malaysian furniture industry, some of the biggest strides have been made in the utilization of rubberwood (*Hevea brasiliensis*). The rubber tree, initially grown for its latex, is now sought for its light and pliable timber. This in turn alleviates the pressure on natural forests as suppliers of raw materials for the furniture and several other timber based industries such as joinery, MDF and particleboard. In addition to rubberwood, other species used in furniture making are *kembang semangkuk* (*Scaphium* spp.), *nyatoh* and *balau* which are derived from natural forests.

Another sought-after raw material used in furniture is rattan, a non-timber forest product,

MALAYSIAN WOODCARVING

Woodcarving is one of the oldest crafts in Malaysia. During the heyday of the Malay sultanate in the 15th–17th century, woodcarving flourished under royal patronage. Woodcarving became the principal decorative item of traditional Malay palaces and the homes of influential families. Even today, the houses and palaces of old still retain the beautifully carved wooden fittings and furniture, which reflect the exceptional skill and artistry of Malay craftsmen. Common patterns used in woodcarving are the *awan larat* (flowing clouds) and floral motifs.

Terengganu's Tanjong Jara Resort is a very good example of restoration and renovation work undertaken to preserve 17th-century traditional Malay architecture. The resort's architecture is based on that of traditional Malay palaces, which are predominantly timber structures. The style won the resort the coveted Aga Khan Award for Architecture in July 1987. Another Aga Khan Award for Architecture winner is Salinger House. Built almost entirely from *chengal* (*Neobalanocarpus heimii*) timber by traditional craftsmen from the east coast, the house was designed by architect Jimmy Lim for Haji Rudin Salinger. It won the award in 1998.

The office and official residence of the Prime Minister and the Istana Budaya (National Theatre) represent the new generation of modern structures that are extensively embellished with a variety of Malaysian timbers. In Perdana Putra, the Prime Minister's office, *resak* (*Vatica* spp.) is used for

Top: No nails were used in the main structure of Salinger house which took more than six years to build. Traditional architectural concepts were utilized to ensure cross and natural ventilation.
Right: An example of the fine filigree wood carvings that adorn the Istana Kenangan in Perak.

flooring, teak for carvings and *nyatoh* (spp. of Sapotaceae) for furniture, doors and wall panels. B*alau* (*Shorea* spp.), *merbau* (*Instia palembanica*), *nyatoh*, *rengas* (*Gluta* spp.), *mempisang* (spp. of Annonaceae), *geronggang* (*Cratoxylum* spp.) and damar minyak (*Agathis borneensis*) were used in the construction of the Istana Budaya.

A unique feature of traditional Malay timber architecture is that it is both decorative and functional—timber grilles, fanlights and dividers break up large areas that receive direct sunlight into smaller ones so that the interior remains cool without compromising on natural lighting.
Above: Decorative grilles in Salinger house.
Middle: A master woodcarver at work.
Left: The timber-based reception area at award-winning Tanjong Jara Resort.

which can be made into attractive tropical-style furniture. Traditional and contemporary designs, which are both ergonomic and creative, have won the acceptance of overseas buyers seeking furniture for the home, office and the outdoors at exhibitions such as the annual Malaysian International Furniture Fair (MIFF). While Malaysian furniture has had good appeal in America and Japan, market penetration into Europe and the Middle East is progressing well.

Malaysia also enjoys a strong reputation in the BCJ market; it is one of the leading exporters of joinery products such as doors, windows, facades and flooring. This industry too, has made impressive progress in 2001, earning RM695.6 million (USD183 million) in export compared to RM338.9 million (USD135.1 million) in 1995. Species leading the charge in this front are the *meranti*, *merbau*, *keruing*, *nyatoh*, *bintangor* (*Calophyllum* spp.), *jelutong* (*Dyera costulata*) and rubberwood. Dark red *meranti* is especially favoured in The Netherlands, Germany and the UK, where this durable reddish brown timber is recognized as an excellent material for heavy duty usage such as building exteriors. Another European favourite is the *merbau*, a heavy hardwood that is even more versatile—it is suitable for high quality joinery as well as interior panelling, strip and parquet flooring and decorative work.

Dark red *meranti* is a popular choice for building exteriors such as window frames in Europe.

In 1995, the Joiners' Trade Guild in the German city of Mannheim acknowledged tropical timbers as being most suitable for use as window frames because of their excellent woodworking properties, versatility and pleasing appearance. They are found to be extremely stable, durable and strong. At the Bouwbeurs 1997 International Building and Construction Exhibition, the largest of its kind in The Netherlands, *merbau* received equal billing with temperate species such as maple (Aceraceae), ash (Oleaceae) and beech (Fagaceae) for use in staircases.

Malaysian joinery products have also penetrated other international markets. Flooring in the form of solid strips, parquet strips and the innovative three-layer pre-finished flooring tiles or strips have found world-wide acceptance in the United States, United Kingdom, Japan and Australia. Apart from their pleasing

A highly versatile material, rattan can be used to produce stylish furniture.

BOAT BUILDING, THE TERENGGANU WAY

Malaysia has a centuries-old tradition in boat building, which dates back to the days when fishing was one of the main economic activities. With an abundance

The boat builders of Terengganu are adept at building wooden fishing vessels.

of timber available, the preferred choice for both the hull and deck of the boats is the heavy hardwood *chengal* (*Neobalanocarpus heimii*).

The state of Terengganu on the east coast of the Peninsula has distinguished itself as the premier site for quality boat building, centred in Pulau Duyung. It is a skill that the boat builders inherited from their forefathers. The old fishing vessels reflect Arab and European influences as well as the local environment; the prow sports the *bangau* or cattle egret (*Bubulcus ibis*), a common migratory bird in this area, or the mythical *garuda*.

The traditional way of boat building is unconventional as the hull of the

vessel is built first, followed by the frames. The planks are first secured to the ground and progressively shaped with the aid of small fires. The hull is then constructed with the use of edge dowels spaced along the plank's length before the frames are built and fitted internally. What makes the traditional method of building a boat unique is that the builder is guided exclusively by memory and experience. No sketches, no plans and few mistakes.

---

aesthetic appeal, these products have gained ground because they are easy to install, durable, and require minimum maintenance—all strong selling points.

Wood panel products, which are also lucrative exports, initially consisted primarily of plywood and blockboard. Besides supplying plywood for construction and export, the plywood industry has ventured into value-added products for interior fittings, furniture and joinery. Tougher plywood such as concrete formwork and marine plywood are designed to tolerate harsh weather conditions. On the other end of the scale are decorative panels finished either in wood veneers or synthetic laminates such as melamine.

Particleboard, another important panel product, is made exclusively from wood. It is much sought-after in the manufacture of kitchen cabinets, mobile homes, partitions, furniture and home fittings. The strong and sturdy boards have smooth surfaces that lend themselves well to painting or lamination. Those made of woodchip and cement, known as cement boards, have the additional advantage of being fire- and termite-resistant. A more recent arrival is the Medium Density Fibreboard (MDF) industry that made its presence felt only in the 1990s. MDF is produced mainly from smaller logs and branchwood of the rubber tree. Larger logs are used for sawntimber. Its attractive straw colour and ease-of-machining make MDF a highly desirable material for joinery and furniture. Indeed, Malaysia is one of the leading exporters of raw

Part of the operations at a plywood factory.

and finished MDF, which contributed RM873.2 million (USD 229.8 million) to export sales in 2001.

The rainforest also yields an assortment of non-timber products, which have since time immemorial provided man with food, shelter, convenience goods and cultural artifacts that can be used for the home, work and leisure. Of the thousands of plant types in the forest, bamboo, rattan and the nipa palm are among the most widely utilized.

In Malaysia, there are altogether 80 species of bamboo, which grow in the fringe of the rainforest. Some are native and several are introduced, with only a handful dominating home usage and cottage industries. The ubiquitous bamboo is raw material for boat and home construction, fishing rods and traps, bridges, pipes, fence palings, laundry poles, vegetable and fishing stakes, bird cages, poultry coops, winnowing trays, buckets, storage bins, food carriers and covers, torch holders, satay sticks, joss sticks, decorative and personal ornaments; even surgical and musical instruments.

Bamboo is exploited commercially for the manufacture of poultry cages, vegetable baskets, incense and joss sticks, skewers, chopsticks and sun blinds. Favoured species for these products are *Gigantochloa scortechinii* and *G. wrayi*, which occur in large quantities in disturbed forests, sometimes together with other bamboo species. There is now a move towards commercializing production further; to meet growing demand, development of bamboo forest plantations has been initiated. Bamboo has already proven its versatility as furniture and parquet flooring material.

Rattan (*Calamus* spp.) shares a somewhat similar history with bamboo, and is a choice material for high-end and sophisticated furniture. Malaysia is the custodian of 200 out of the 600 known species of rattan in the world. It is traditionally used in cordage, basketry, fish traps, food and medicine. The thorny leaf sheaths on the stems are removed to expose smooth cane, which is strong and flexible and ideal for binding. The smoother outer skin is the foundation of the weavecraft tradition of Malaysia's indigenous people, who fashion it into baskets, hats, mats and ceremonial costumes.

Once tapped exclusively for latex, rubber trees (*Hevea brasiliensis*) are now also felled for their light and pliable timber.

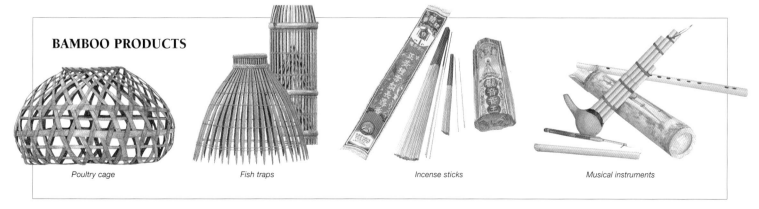

BAMBOO PRODUCTS

Poultry cage   *Fish traps*   *Incense sticks*   *Musical instruments*

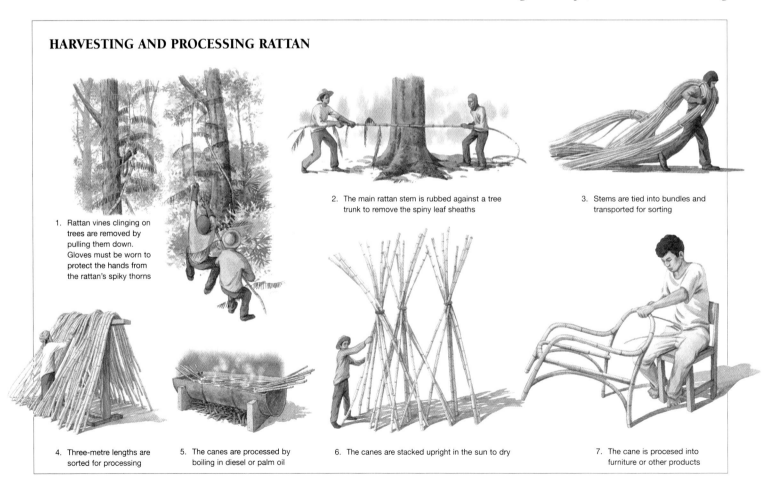
Rattan is used in many types of furniture.

Most intriguing is the *rawai* or *sabit*, a bodice that is part of the ceremonial dress of Iban and Kanowit women. This is Sarawak's answer to the West's whalebone corset. The *rawai* consists of hoops of rattan held together by brass or silver rings and is worn across the torso to accentuate the feminine shape of the wearer (*see p138*).

Commercially, the most important rattan species is *Calamus manan*, which is best for furniture making. An estimated 15,000 people, mainly Orang Asli, are involved in collecting rattan from the forests of Peninsular Malaysia. Malaysia has taken some positive action to stimulate the rattan products industry which includes the cultivation of rattan to augment the supply of these raw materials.

Even more versatile is the nipa palm (*Nypa fruticans*). Every bit of this mangrove resident can be harvested for a variety of uses. The trunk is used for house construction while the fronds are commonly used as thatch and in weavecraft. The fibres of the leaf midribs are soaked and twisted into rope, which is used in the home and for boat construction. Fishermen use the leaf petioles as floats for fishing nets while the stiff midribs of the fronds are used in making fish traps, fish fences and fishing

HARVESTING AND PROCESSING RATTAN

1. Rattan vines clinging on trees are removed by pulling them down. Gloves must be worn to protect the hands from the rattan's spiky thorns

2. The main rattan stem is rubbed against a tree trunk to remove the spiny leaf sheaths

3. Stems are tied into bundles and transported for sorting

4. Three-metre lengths are sorted for processing

5. The canes are processed by boiling in diesel or palm oil

6. The canes are stacked upright in the sun to dry

7. The cane is procesed into furniture or other products

rods. The outer layers of the leaf stalk yield pulp suitable for good quality boards. The tremendous value of this common palm has not gone unnoticed and commercial exploitation of this species is being explored. Its role in rainforest and rural communities, however, is on the decline.

The versatile nipa palm (*Nypa fruticans*) is used as a building material, particularly for roof thatch, by rural communities.

Forest giants are more than just timber producers; they have multiple uses. While timber is the most commercially lucrative part of the tree, their nuts, buds, leaves and bark have had a long history as traditional sources of food, resin and oil. The biggest provider of benefits in this regard are the mighty dipterocarps. The egg-shaped nuts of *Shorea* species such as *sengkawang* (*S. sumatrana*) are a delicacy in Sarawak, where the kernels are eaten with rice. The nuts are also processed into cooking oil. Meanwhile, the fat is extracted to produce illipe butter, which has gained tremendous commercial favour among chocolate manufacturers in Europe and Japan who use it as a substitute for highly priced cocoa butter.

Another by-product of several species of trees is resin. To collect the resin, notches are cut into the tree, allowing the resin to be released. Once it has hardened, the resin is scraped off and taken away to be graded according to the colour, firmness and opacity. *Damar minyak* (*Agathis borneensis*) produces a clear white resin and the *chengal* (*Neobalanocarpus heimii*) yields the high-grade *damar penak*. Another high light-coloured, clear resin is the *damar luis* from the *Hopea* species while the *keruing* (*Dipterocarpus* spp.) and *resak* (*Cotylelobium* spp. and *Vatica* spp.) are the source of oleoresins, a combination of resins and essential oils. All these resins formed the basis of a small-scale resin export industry in the early 20th century, when they were sought for lacquer production. The Great Depression of the 1930s put paid to all this. Plunging markets sent the industry into a spin from which it never recovered. Other export products such as tin and rubber were found to be more viable as revenue earners. Today, a small volume of resin is produced, serving mainly traditional functions such as termite repellent, wood varnish and as a waterproof filler for boats. Another useful material was the latex from the bark of the *jelutong* (*Dyera costulata*). The latex was used for the manufacture of chewing gum and rubber goods.

Resin oozing out from the *meranti rambai daun* (*Shorea accuminata*). Resins are used mainly in insect repellents, wood varnishes and grouting.

USEFUL PRODUCTS FROM THE FOREST

1. **Leaves** - Medicines, perfumes, dyes, food and flavouring extracts
2. **Bark** - Flavouring, tannin, gums, resins, perfumes, medicines and dyes
3. **Stumps** - Fuelwood, furniture and novelty items
4. **Logs** - Particleboard, fibreboard, sawntimber and veneer/plywood
5. **Branchwood** - Particleboard, fibreboard, sawntimber and fuelwood

NOT TO SCALE

'Kemenyan sebesar lutut, jika tiada terbakar manakan berbau?'
A piece of benzoin may be as large as your knee, but if you do not burn it how are you to get at its fragrance?

MALAY PROVERB MEANING MANY THINGS ARE USELESS IF HOARDED, AND ONLY USEFUL IF USED.

The most famous of resins must surely be Bornean camphor, which occurs in cavities in the trunk of the *kapur* (*Dryobalanops aromatica*). The strong odour works well as an insect repellent, making this timber a highly desirable construction material for clothes chests, in the past. Another fragrant resin is the *Styrax benzoin*, known locally as *kemenyan*, which the 14th-century Moroccan traveller Ibn Batuta labelled the 'Java frankincense' because of its similarity to the biblical frankincense. It is obtained after bruising the bark of the tall, heavily-buttressed tree *Styrax benzoin*, and has a well-established record as an antiseptic in both Eastern and Western folk medicine. Benzoin tinctures are used as preservatives in medicinal and cosmetic preparations, while benzoic acid figures prominently in traditional Chinese medicine. The resin also has religious significance; it is burnt as incense at Muslim, Christian and Hindu religious ceremonies.

Another fragrant wood is *gaharu* (*Aquilaria malaccensis*). Oil from the *gaharu* is highly prized by Western perfumeries, because of its ability to retain scent. Even more glamorous is the role of the *kenanga* (*Cananga odorata*), better known as ylang-ylang. The essential oil from the fragrant clusters of yellow-green flowers from the droopy 30-metre high *kenanga* is widely used in the perfume industry.

Fragrant oils produced from spices such as cinnamon (*Cinnamomum zeylanicum*), cloves (*Syzygium caryophyllus*) and nutmeg (*Myristica fragrans*) caused Europeans to rush to the East in the 1500s, in a mad scramble to establish colonies in the 'Spice Islands' of the East Indies. Spices were then the only known food preservative. Most of these spices are used in cooking and are also common ingredients in traditional and modern medicines. The oils from nutmeg and pepper (*Piper nigrum*) are popular in perfumes. Plant oils are also used in household products such as candles and soap.

Impregnable mangrove swamps may be the most uncongenial of places for human habitation, but they rate highly as a profit-making zone, especially from species that yield tannins and resins for the production of ink, detergents and rubber glues. The *Rhizophora* sp. wood's high tannin content makes it ideal for construction purposes;

the tannin prevents the wood from rotting. By far, the most important tannin producer is *bakau kurap* (*R. mucronata*), which has an average height of 30 metres and a 60-centimetre diameter girth. Tannin or tannic acid extracted from its bark is used to produce leather tanning solutions, fabric dyes and ink. The extract is also useful in the oil industry; tannic acid helps reduce the viscosity of mud when drilling for oil.

A pepper smallholding in Sarawak. Malaysian exports of pepper exceed exports of any other spice.

Taking the first step towards mobilizing the resources of botanists, zoologists, chemists, biochemists and enthno-botanists to investigate and document its rich biological heritage that may hold the key to some medical cures, the State Legislative Assembly of the state of Sarawak passed the Sarawak Biodiversity Bill in December 1997 to set up the Sarawak Biodiversity Centre. This resource centre became a reality a year later. At the top of the agenda is the scientific investigation and documentation of the rich flora and fauna of the state. This, in turn, provides tremendous opportunities to the centre to play a significant role in conserving and sustainably utilizing the biological heritage of the state.

In April 1997, the American biotechnology firm MediChem Research announced its plan to develop the natural drug Calanolide A, a compound obtained from the *bintangor* (*Calophyllum lanigerum*), a tree that grows wild in the rainforests of Malaysia. Preliminary laboratory tests have demonstrated that Calanolide A stops the AIDS virus from reproducing and is effective in preventing mutations of the virus which could not be halted by chemically engineered drugs. Since mid-1999 *bintangor* extracts have been

THE SARAWAK BIODIVERSITY CENTRE

The Sarawak Biodiversity Centre was set up in 1998 in the spirit of the Convention on Biological Diversity, primarily to ensure that the wealth of the resource-rich rainforest is conserved well, used sustainably and shared equitably by current and potential users. Threats to biodiversity from habitat loss and over-exploitation will also be reduced.

The centre sets out to be the focal point and world class resource centre of Sarawak's rainforest biodiversity by establishing a comprehensive biodiversity inventory and undertaking monitoring, research, education, utilization and management of the vast forest resources of the state.

Its primary tasks are to:
- Promote awareness and appreciation for Sarawak's rich biodiversity among all sectors of society to ensure its conservation
- Obtain and disseminate accurate and up-to-date information on all aspects of biodiversity in Sarawak
- Identify, set priorities and initiate programmes for research and utilization of biological resources in Sarawak including bio-prospecting and product development
- Establish links with similar local and foreign institutions
- Plan and initiate programmes for the conservation and protection of biological resources in Sarawak

The easily accessible Bako National Park on the estuary of the Sarawak River. Proper documentation of existing species will help promote the sustainable use of such species.

tested on AIDS patients in Kuala Lumpur, Singapore and the United States to enable scientists and doctors to familiarize themselves with treatment procedures and monitor the success rate. This discovery is a milestone for the tropical rainforest, which has been hailed as a major source for herbal medical cures.

According to the Forest Research Institute Malaysia (FRIM), 39 out of the 95 plant species used to produce 121 clinically common drugs in the world originate from tropical rainforests. In 1997, herbal medicines fetched RM111.6 billion (USD40 billion) in global sales and

R&D remains a top priority in forestry both for timber and non-timber products; leading the way is FRIM (above).

the figure is growing rapidly. Apart from their use in pharmaceuticals, herbal medicines, cosmetics, personal care and biochemical products, tropical plant extracts are also increasingly sought-after by the burgeoning billion-ringgit herbal and medicinal plant industry. In Malaysia, this market has registered steady growth, with a current value of RM1.2 billion (USD315 million) compared to RM60 million (USD23.8 million) in 1996.

Biotechnology has become a high-growth industry. The Malaysian Industry-Government Group for High Technology (MIGHT) was formed to prospect for business opportunities through strategic exploration of technology for attainment of Malaysia's Vision 2020 objectives. Following that trend, in 2002, biotechnology in Malaysia was boosted by the setting up of three biotechnology research and development centres—the Institute for Genomics and Molecular Biology, the Institute for Pharmaceuticals and Natraceuticals and the Institute of Agricultural Biotechnology. These research centres will be temporarily housed in local institutions before moving to their permanent home in BioValley in the Multimedia Super Corridor, Malaysia's information superhighway.

The World Health Organization estimates that 80 per cent of the population in developing countries rely on traditional medicine for their primary health care needs. In Malaysia, there has been a revival in the use of traditional medicine and a move to integrate natural remedies with conventional Western medicines. There is also a parallel move to commercialize the cultivation of medicinal plants. As a result, the country's first herbal monograph was launched on 15 June 1999. Entitled *Malaysian Herbal Monograph Volume One*, it contains comprehensive information on 20 local medicinal plants which will be invaluable in helping set up plantations to cultivate relevant species instead of resorting to a haphazard exploitation of wild plants in their natural setting.

Traditional medicine was historically dispensed by native medicine men. In multi-ethnic Malaysia, there are several types of medicine men. The *bomoh* or *pawang* is the fount of Malay medical remedies, with the *bidan*, always a mature lady, in a supporting role as the village midwife. The Chinese have

OPPOSITE: Timber was used extensively in the construction of this house.

Given the wealth of its natural heritage, Malaysia is well-positioned to lead the way in biotechnology, which has been accorded high-priority status under the 8th Malaysia Plan (2000–04).

Kacip Fatimah (Labisia pumila), the 'lady's herb', is widely used in traditional medicine to prevent pre- and post-natal ailments.

their *sinseh* and the Indians, their Ayurvedic practitioner. But the borders between the three types of medicine men are becoming blurred as Malaysians seek out the best of traditional cures.

Riding high on the list of herbal remedies is *tongkat Ali (Eurycoma longifolia)* (Ali's walking stick), which has reached adulation point among Malaysian males because of its reputation as an efficacious aphrodisiac.

Kacip Fatimah (Labisia pumila), a common small woody plant can be used in a number of remedies for ladies. A decoction of *kacip Fatimah* is used to hasten the delivery of babies and is recommended for postnatal recovery. This herb, which translates literally as Fatimah's *areca* nut slicer, is also used to treat gonorrhoea, dysentery, flatulence and burping. Another postnatal remedy is found in the herb commonly known as *kemoyang (Homalomena sagittifolia)*. The leaves of this aromatic forest herb are used to wrap a heated stone which is used to massage the abdomen after childbirth. This practice is believed to hasten the contraction of the womb and revitalize circulation. The leaves and roots can be boiled to make a tea that reduces high fever.

Some of these age-old herbal remedies evolved as a result of common ailments afflicting rural and forest communities. The rainforest also provides an assortment of cures for malaria, smallpox, diarrhoea, constipation, haemorrhoids, bruises, boils, sores, cuts, insect bites, skin itches, ringworm, ulcers and influenza. Most of these remedies lie in the hands of just two dozen species. This clutch includes *putrawali (Tinospora crispa)*, *pulai (Alstonia scholaris)*, the *bidara* tree *(Ziziphus mauritiana)*, *tepus tanah (Zingiber spectabile)*, *gelenggang besar (Senna alata)*, the Portia tree or Pacific rosewood *(Thespesia populnea)*, *terong pipit (Solanum torvum)*,

Tongkat Ali (Eurycoma longifolia)

TONGKAT ALI

The root of the five-metre-high tree, which grows wild in the forest, is said to increase the male libido. It is freely available and is sold in its raw form in the *pasar* (market) and modern supermarkets. *Tongkat Ali* is also sold as a canned drink, with tea and coffee flavours, in most wayside restaurants and at 24-hour convenience stores. The roots can also be mixed with the oil of *buah keras* and raw rice to produce an ointment that relieves abdominal pain and fever. An infusion of *tongkat ali* roots is imbibed as a tonic to revive the strength of women after childbirth. The leaves are used to treat cuts and heal wounds, or ground into a paste and applied on the forehead to relieve headaches.

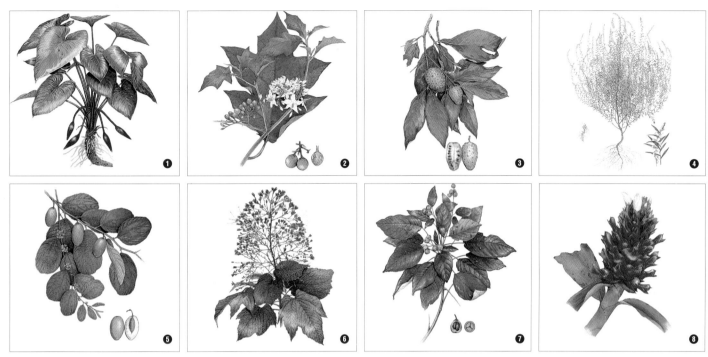

Some medicinal herbs from the forest:

1. *Homalomena sagittifolia*
2. *Solanum torvum*
3. *Morinda citrifolia*
4. *Polygala paniculata*
5. *Ziziphus mauritiana*
6. *Clerodendron paniculatum*
7. *Croton argyratus*
8. *Costus speciosus*

mengkudu (*Morinda citrifolia*), *Polygala paniculata*, *mengkeh* (*Croton argyratus*) and *ketapang* (*Terminalia catappa*).

Some species in this group of plants are being studied for their propensity to relieve modern-day ailments such as high blood pressure and diabetes. One plant that deserves special mention is *hempedu bumi* (*Andrographis paniculata*) which contains the bitter chemical component furanoditerpene. Once used to treat fever and snake bites, *hempedu bumi* (bile of the earth) is being increasingly recommended for the treatment of diabetes, high blood pressure, chest pain and tonsillitis by native medicine practitioners. In fact, this herb is widely cultivated in China, India and more recently in Malaysia.

Modern trends in medicine, research and consumer preferences have fuelled the demand for herbal remedies. This has resulted in a sharp demand for raw materials from the rainforest to produce pharmaceuticals, vitamins, minerals and health foods. The Malaysian government realizes that uncontrolled collection of raw materials can lead to the destruction of forest species while the wrong identification of species could have dire consequences for the consumer. To prevent this, Malaysia's 3rd National Agriculture Policy calls for the sustainable usage of the country's biological resources. Through ongoing research, it has identified plants for commercialization—medicinal plants that can be cultivated as an agricultural crop, thus leaving most of the wealth of the forest to grow and replenish itself according to the natural specifications of Mother Nature.

An Orang Asli gathering medicinal plants from the rainforest.

CHAPTER SEVEN

MANAGING MALAYSIA'S FORESTS

Malaysia is fortunate to have inherited from the British the legacy of sound forest management, presumably based on lessons learnt in their own country and in some of their colonies. Officially forestry in Malaysia is recorded as having started with the appointment of the first forestry officer just a little more than 100 years ago, on 16 October 1901. This landmark date marked the beginning of planned management of Malaysian forests, acknowledging the role of forests in economic development—timber revenues were used to fund socio-economic development projects.

The early years were known as the 'gutta percha' era (1900–10), when latex from the Palaquium spp. known locally as gutta percha, was a cash cow. One of the best-known insulators of heat, the latex was much sought after in the manufacture of submarine cables, and electrical, surgical and dental apparatus. Not surprisingly, early forest cultivation was confined mainly to the establishment of Palaquium, which fetched as much as RM760 per pikul (equivalent to 60 kilograms) in its heyday. As a result, the trees were destructively felled to obtain their lucrative latex. Meanwhile, logging during this period was highly selective and confined to heavy hardwoods such as chengal (Neobalanocarpus heimii) and balau (Shorea spp.) which were used for railway sleepers that were being laid across the country. To maintain a steady supply of these species, enrichment planting was undertaken, especially of chengal.

Lygodium longifolia leaf.

The great demand for heavy hardwoods heralded the Improvement and Regeneration Felling Era (1911–42), when 'improved felling' was practised on forest reserves that were opened for logging. The branches of unwanted or 'interfering species' were pruned so that the heavy hardwoods could grow unencumbered, receiving their proper quota of light and space, and eventually yield good harvests. Put simply, the felling improved the chances of survival of heavy hardwoods at the expense of other species in the vicinity. Moreover, this also helped regenerate a new rich crop of the chosen species. These unwanted timbers found themselves in favour as fuelwood in rubber factories and as poles in tin mines during the rubber and tin boom.

OPPOSITE: Forestry involves surveying, inventory of the forest and sustainably managing the forest ecosystem.

Treating railway sleepers
at FRIM, c. 1961.

A. M. Burn-Murdoch, the Conservator of
Forest for the Straits Settlements and
the Federated Malay States in 1901.

There was a discernible shift in logging practices in the aftermath of
the Second World War. Market conditions had changed and timber was now
sought as raw material by sawmills, which required a reliable supply of timber.
As a result, the Malayan Uniform System (MUS) emerged. It involved converting
the rich, complex, multi-species and multi-aged virgin forests into a more or less
even-aged forest containing a greater proportion of commercial species. To achieve this,
all commercial species above 45 centimetres in diameter at breast height were felled in
one single logging operation. Silvicultural treatment followed, with climber-cutting and
poison-girdling of defective trees or non-commercial trees as small as five centimetres in
diameter. The growth of favoured species was the foremost priority under this
management system. The logged area was then left for 60 to 80 years to regrow for the
next harvest. Undertaken over large tracts in different parts of the country at different
times, the MUS was based on uniformity of the species that would be logged. The
success of this system depended very much on the abundance, distribution, and survival
of seedlings and saplings of economic species. As a management system, MUS was
considered successful at regenerating large tracts of lowland dipterocarp forests.

MUS, however, was not fully applicable on hill forests. Since 1978 MUS has
gradually been replaced by the Selective Management System (SMS), heralding the

age of multiple-use forest management. The main difference between MUS and SMS is the length of the harvesting cycle. The former depends on seedlings and saplings for future harvest—trees to be logged are identified at seedling stage and harvesting occurs almost 60 years later when these 'babies' are fully grown. SMS short circuits the cutting cycle by zeroing in on medium-sized trees with 30–45 centimetre diameter for the next harvest, thus reducing waiting time for the next harvest. Forest inventories, cutting limits, timber tagging, felling, buffer zones, post-logging forest surveys and silvicultural treatments are all common currency under both systems.

The cornerstone of SMS is the flexibility of harvesting regimes and its economically and ecologically friendly methods. It has paved the way for more complex and sophisticated forest management before, during and after harvest; activities at every stage have to be clearly defined, planned, implemented and monitored for SMS to work well.

Beginning in the 1970s, forestry became a contentious issue. Tropical forestry in particular became the target of attack by environmentalists, some of whom chose to

Sustainable forest management involves the measurement and labelling of trees.

Regenerated forests restore the balance to degraded environment.

BASIC PRINCIPLES OF TROPICAL FOREST MANAGEMENT

1. Forests are dynamic. If not utilized, trees are continually dying and being replaced. Sustainable utilization systems are viable so long as they mimic natural forest dynamics and work within the nutrient limitations of the ecosystem. This has to be taken into account in forest management.

2. Forests provide a wide variety of goods and services. Non-timber products such as fruits, nuts, resins and rattan are often harvested by forest-dwellers and provide economic benefits that can be more valuable than timber removal. Economic analysis of the value of timber harvesting must consider the potential threat to these opportunities for the community.

3. Timber should realize its true value. Timber prices must cover the environmental and replacement costs. Otherwise there is no incentive to restore forests so that it can be sustained at its productive capacity. Governments generally collect far too little forest revenue to reinvest in replacement efforts. Also, when there is no incentive for loggers to utilize low grade and waste products, sustainability could be endangered by high grading and forest fires (fuelled by dry matter left behind after logging operations).

4. Fiscal and financial incentives for conservation and regeneration must be provided. Just as logging should bear its environmental costs, conservation, regeneration and reforestation should enjoy profits from the environmental benefits they convey to the society at large.

Adapted from the CURE (Conservation, Utilization, Reforestation and Education) Programme of the International Wood Products Association (IHPA) of USA. CURE was established in 1988 to protect tropical forests and the international timber trade.

In Malaysia, enrichment planting is undertaken in poorly stocked areas; value is added by planting species common to the area.

wage a personal and passionate war against loggers. Their stand was based on the claim that tropical forests are carbon sinks; removing them was considered tantamount to destabilizing global climate by accelerating global warming.

This argument, however, has been proven to be flawed by respected eco-scientists such as Patrick Moore, the co-founder of Greenpeace, and Philip Stott, a professor of biogeography at the School of Oriental and African Studies in London and editor of the *Journal of Biogeography*. Both started as conventional environmentalists but in the 1980s and 1990s each independently began to dig deeper into the 'save the rainforest' issue. Separately, they arrived at remarkably similar conclusions: public opinion was wrong. Stott strikes a blow to the carbon sink theory. *'This lungs of the earth business is nonsense; the daftest of all theories. In fact, because trees fall down and decay, rainforests actually take in slightly more oxygen than they give out. The idea of them soaking in carbon dioxide and giving out oxygen is a myth. It is only fast growing young trees that actually take up carbon dioxide. Also, in terms of world systems, rainforests are basically irrelevant. World weather is governed by the oceans—that great system of ocean atmospherics. Most things that happen on land are mere blips to the system, basically insignificant.'*

These findings, published in the *Washington Post* in the year 2000, represent a discernible shift in professional opinion on tropical forestry in the closing years of

OPPOSITE: A settlement on the fringes of the forest.

'...we must also ensure that our valuable natural resource is not wasted. Our land must remain productive and fertile, our atmosphere clear and clean, our water unpolluted, our forest resources capable of regeneration, able to yield the needs of our national development. The beauty of our land must not be desecrated—for its own sake and for our economic advancement.'

– DATO' SERI DR MAHATHIR MOHAMAD, THE PRIME MINISTER OF MALAYSIA EXCERPT FROM VISION 2020, THE BLUEPRINT FOR MALAYSIA'S PROGRESS TOWARDS DEVELOPED COUNTRY STATUS (1992).

SUSTAINABLE FORESTRY MANAGEMENT PRACTICES IN MALAYSIA

1. Annual coupe: The number of trees allowed to be harvested is determined using SFM practices

2. Pre-felling inventory. The number and size of trees are recorded

3. Selective harvesting using directional felling to reduce impact takes place according to national allowances*

4. Post-felling inventory. If necessary, silvicultural treatment is applied

5. Regenerated forest after 25–60 years

* National allowances: 32 residual trees of above 30 centimetres diameter at breast height (dbh) to form the next crop

Minimum cutting limit: dipterocarps–55 centimetres dbh, non-dipterocarps–45 centimetres dbh

Source: MTC: Forestry Practices in Malaysia

the 20th century. However, they came many years too late for many tropical timber producers, who had been subject to bad press, boycotts and bans in the international marketplace. As an important exporter of tropical timbers, Malaysia had by then embarked on its journey of sustainable forestry management to meet the International Tropical Timber Organization (ITTO) Year 2000 Objective that all tropical timber traded internationally should be obtained from sustainable sources.

In Malaysia, ITTO first made its presence felt in 1988, with the project entitled *'Forest Management of Natural Forest in Malaysia'* that concentrated on the development of appropriate forest management systems that would bring equitable returns to forest owners and loggers without compromising on forest sustainability. The project studied the response of residual stands under various management regimes in two virgin forest reserves—the Lesong Forest Reserve in Pahang and the Sungai Lalang Forest Reserve in Selangor. It also studied the regeneration capacity of dipterocarp forest under various silvicultural treatments in two logged-over forests in Keldang Saiong Forest Reserve in Perak and the Cherul Forest Reserve in Terengganu.

The second project, called *'Rehabilitation of Natural Forest'* involved studies of natural regeneration and silvicultural treatments including tree planting in degraded forest areas of the Korbu Forest Reserve in Perak between 1993–99.

In Labis Forest Reserve in Johor, the logged forest was conserved and rehabilitated with enrichment planting in 1999. A joint Malaysia-ITTO project, it involved upgrading the nursery and establishment of two seed production areas.

Information technology has revolutionized forestry practices in Malaysia.

The 208.9-hectare site was planted with propagated *meranti tembaga* (*Shorea leprosula*), *meranti kepong* (*Shorea ovalis*), *meranti sarang punai* (*Shorea parvifolia*), *meranti rambai daun* (*Shorea acuminata*), *meranti temak nipis* (*Shorea roxburghii*), and *merawan siput jantan* (*Hopea odorata*).

A Model Forest Management Area (MFMA) project was undertaken in Sarawak in 1993, covering 162,000 hectares across the Sibu and Bintulu divisions. The area is a microcosm of Sarawak's 8.9 million hectares of hill forests. The project set out to demonstrate that tropical timber harvesting, when properly managed, does not damage beyond recovery the ecology or the forest resource itself. Forestry department and logging company staff were trained in all planning, operational and monitoring aspects, especially of hill forests. Research and development in harvesting technologies and appropriate silvicultural methods were applied for planning and monitoring of forestry operations. New environmentally friendly technology was introduced—helicopter logging, Geographical Information System (GIS) and heli-borne digital video graphing. There was also community involvement, with the logging industry and the public invited to participate in sustainable forest management.

In 1996, the Forestry Department reported that Sarawak had reduced its annual log production from 12.5 million cubic metres in 1992 to 9.4 million cubic metres.

Established in 1983 by a United Nations-negotiated agreement, the ITTO promotes sustainable forest development through trade, conservation and best-practice forest management.

TECHNOLOGY-AIDED FORESTRY MANAGEMENT

In the past few decades, forest mapping was primarily based on aerial photographs and field inventories. But Sustainable Forest Management (SFM) practices require more regular and efficient mapping and monitoring of the forests for effective planning, management and conservation of forest resources.

Conventional forest mapping was time consuming in Malaysia given the dense and extensive forest cover across the country. The advent of remote satellite sensors with relatively high resolution images and high-powered data processing computers are gaining common currency as reliable and efficient forest mapping and monitoring tools.

A FAO study conducted in 1989 recommended that the Forestry Department of Peninsular Malaysia (FDPM) adopt the usage of satellite imagery and the Geographical Information System (GIS) for forest monitoring. With technical assistance from the ASEAN Institute of Forest Management and the European Union, a GIS and Mapping section was set up at FDPM and GIS mapping made its debut in Malaysia in 1990.

A computer-based system, GIS provides four sets of capabilities to handle geo-referenced data:
• Input
• Data management (storage)
• Manipulation and analysis
• Output

The next phase of GIS mapping in Malaysia will see the integration of this spatial database with the non-spatial Management Information System of the FDPM. This will enable forest planners and managers at all levels and from different states to have easy access to up-to-date information at the flick of a computer terminal switch.

1. GIS Forest Monitoring: The satellite captures forest images

2. The satellite transmits the images to the receiving station

3. The images are analysed, stored and used for planning and management of forests

Dr Stephan Andel, MFMA consultant and project leader, also delivered some good news: forestry practices in Sarawak were going in the right direction. He said that from the project's studies, there was no hard evidence of relative decline in flora and game fauna in certain logged areas of the MFMA; instead, some game fauna may even have increased.

Several models have been established across Malaysia. In Sabah, the Malaysian-German Sustainable Forest Management (SFM) Project on a 100,000-hectare forest reserve within the Deramakot and Segaliud Lokan Forest Reserves in Sandakan was identified as the model for all forest reserves in the state. This project involved developing the area using integrated multiple-use management planning. Multiple-use planning takes into account the diverse functions of the forest, ranging from protection of soil, water and biodiversity, recreation for the urban population and the production of non-wood products in rural areas. It is, in effect, socially, ecologically and scientifically acceptable. The project also saw the introduction of the skyline system to extract timber from Sabah's remote forests in 1996. This new method minimizes the effects of logging on the environment.

Modern technology and ecofriendly logging practices aside, Malaysia is rigorous about reafforesting and rehabilitating its forests. Again, this has been undertaken with the help of international expertise and in accordance with SFM guidelines. The Forestry Department of Peninsular Malaysia (FDPM) worked with the Japan International Cooperation Agency (JICA) to collect data to develop a Multi-Storied Forest Management Project (MSFM), which was to be adopted as a model for establishing large-scale forest plantations as well as encouraging forest rehabilitation.

This MSFM model involved 1,000 hectares of forest in the state of Perak. Studies were conducted in the forest plantation at Chikus Forest Reserve and the natural forest in Kinta Forest Reserve between 1991 and 1999. It led to the establishment of a mixed forest that is environmentally benign and resistant to pests and plant diseases. The project also produced several important findings. Most significant was the identification of a total of 61 species of high quality trees suitable for planting in both forest plantations and over-logged forests.

Other SFM collaborations include aerial photography, satellite data and development of a

Low impact logging in hill forests:
ABOVE: Heli-logging in Sarawak.

BELOW: Skyline logging in Sabah.

INSET: In the 1990s, the Chikus Forest Reserve in Perak was used as a model for a study on the establishment of large forest plantations and forest rehabilitation.

OPPOSITE: A *batai* (*Paraserianthes falcataria*) plantation. *Batai* is grown in plantations in Sabah and Peninsular Malaysia.

Directional felling ensures that a falling tree does little damage to seedlings or trees growing in the vicinity.

The Malaysian-German Sustainable Forest Management Project in the Deramakot Forest Reserve in Sabah is to be used as a model for all forest management units in the state.

computerized planning system for effective management of mangrove and peatswamps with the Swedish International Development Cooperation Agency and the planting material procurement programme with the German Agency for Technical Corporation (GTZ). An ongoing GTZ project is the Sustainable Management and Conservation Project, which involves updating silvicultural practices, forest management planning guidelines and the economic assessment of SFM. It is also providing technical support for Management Information System (MIS) development in FDPM. The Danish Cooperation for Environment and Development (DANCED), meanwhile, was involved in three projects: sustainable peatswamp management, an integrated plan for sustainable use of mangrove swamps and a study on the extraction and processing of forest residues and small dimension logs.

Meanwhile, several steps in research and development and technology have filtered through to Malaysian forestry, mainly through joint collaboration projects with a few European countries and Japan. A major worldwide trend in forest harvesting since the 1970s has been increased mechanization, which tends to maximize economic efficiency

efficiency and minimize environmental impacts. Increased mechanization is only marginally more expensive than traditional methods. Numerous initiatives and trials have been carried out by the Forest Research Institute Malaysia (FRIM) and other organizations such as GTZ, the Japan International Research Centre for Agricultural Sciences (JIRCAS) and FDPM. Included among the logging methods for hilly areas that have been tried and tested are the 'long haulage ground cable system' (LHGCS) and the 'skyline yarding system', both of which mimimize damage to the environment. The sophisticated reduced-impact heli-logging is only viable in some areas. Other reduced-impact logging practices have been introduced with the use of environmentally friendly machinery such as anti-vibration chainsaws and the A-frame on the rear of the bulldozer. This is undertaken alongside sound logging practices such as proper road alignment, the establishment of buffer zones along waterways and rivers, and directional felling.

These SFM projects involve substantial financial investments. While technical assistance programmes come with funding, it is only partial. In its desire to achieve the ITTO Year 2000 Objective, Malaysia has progressively increased budget allocations for forestry, squarely integrating economic growth with the protection of the environment and natural resources. The expenditure on forest services in Peninsular Malaysia has almost doubled since 1991; it grew from RM125.48 million in 1991 to RM245.5 million in 2000. In Sabah the growth was from RM77.43 million to RM102.25 million; while the allocation for Sarawak rose from RM43.57 million to RM93.12 million for the same period (*see Table 4, p172*). Forest services cover administration, management of national parks, wildlife and bird sanctuaries and research and development. The development expenditure invariably includes projects for research and training, reforestation and rehabilitation, and wildlife and national parks.

'Malaysia is now regarded as one of the tropical countries which take good care of their forests. It manages and maintains them strictly and effectively. Thus, Malaysia can serve as a role model for many other tropical timber producing countries to show how the natural resources can be protected.'

– *MATERIAL UND TECNIK*, 1996
GERMAN MONTHLY
TIMBER TRADE MAGAZINE

LEFT: Reduced-impact logging: the cone at the end of the log aims to minimize forest damage.

RIGHT: Observing the operation of the winch used in the skyline yarding haulage system.

NEXT PAGE: The FDPM provides training in forestry for field staff. This picture shows trainees undergoing practical training on tree identification.

HARVESTING METHODS

Timber harvesting today revolves around reduced- and low-impact logging and transportation. Directional felling ensures that there is minimal damage to the surrounding environment while log haulage involves tractors, trucks and rail transport that have been modified mainly to avoid damage to the forest floor.

3a. Tractor hauling to the log landing site

1. Felling

2. Cross-cutting

3b. Railway transport by locomotive to the log landing site

TABLE 4

MALAYSIAN FOREST SERVICES EXPENDITURE

PENINSULAR MALAYSIA	1991	1995	2000
Forest Administration	56.13	82.11	81.40
Management of national parks, wildlife and bird sanctuaries	15.95	21.76	53.00
Research	14.70	28.69	40.20
Development	38.70	80.42	70.90
TOTAL (RM MILLION)	125.48	212.98	245.50
SABAH	1991	1995	2000
Forest Administration	39.62	45.63	45.45
Management of national parks, wildlife and bird sanctuaries	29.72	20.86	34.02
Research	4.39	4.12	3.76
Development	3.70	15.33	19.02
TOTAL (RM MILLION)	77.43	85.94	102.25
SARAWAK	1991	1995	2000
Forest Administration	26.45	46.20	66.40
Management of national parks, wildlife and bird sanctuaries	2.97	4.10	8.53
Research	2.37	8.10	3.60
Development	11.78	22.43	14.59
TOTAL (RM MILLION)	43.57	80.83	93.12
GRAND TOTAL (RM MILLION)	246.48	379.75	440.87
GRAND TOTAL (USD MILLION)	64.86	99.93	116.02

Source: Forestry Departments of Peninsular Malaysia, Sabah and Sarawak

Funds have also been allocated for the enforcement of environmentally friendly regulations, which includes sustainable forestry. The 2001 Budget provided RM85 million (USD22.3 million) to the Department of Environment, a sum that is more than 2.5 times the RM31.2 million (USD8.2 million) allocated in 1999. In Johor in March 1996, Primary Industries Minister Dato' Seri Lim Keng Yaik said that even though the country was headed for industrialization, it has been able to retain 72 per cent of the total land area under tree and forest cover because of both effective forestry practices and rigorous laws. He said: '*Malaysia's effective implementation of laws and regulations governing logging such as sending illegal loggers to prison has enabled it to preserve its forests.*' Monitoring involves both policing and penalties (*see p175*). Timber concessionaires who subcontract their licences are required to appoint only logging operators registered with the State Forestry Departments.

During the 1995 mid-term review of the progress towards ITTO Year 2000 Objective, Malaysia was identified as one of three countries that was on track to achieve sustainable forest management. More recently, an ITTO report entitled *Review of Progress Towards Year 2000 Objective*, published in November 2000, reaffirmed that Malaysia was one of six countries that appeared 'to be managing some of their forests sustainably at forest management unit level to achieve ITTO Year 2000 Objective'. It said that Malaysia has a system of demarcated permanent forest estates complemented by well-managed networks of totally protected areas with virgin jungle reserves.

5a. Debarked logs are loaded onto a lorry

5c. The logs are transported by road to the mills

4. Debarking of logs

5b. Logs are transported by
river barges to the mills

But this was not the purpose of the Year 2000 Objective. At the November 1998 International Tropical Timber Council session in Yokohama, the then ITTO Executive Director Dr B. C. Y. Freezailah threw some light on the interpretation of the ITTO Objective Year 2000. He said: '*Although the time frame for achieving this objective, Year 2000, is clearly indicated there must also be a linkage of this important commitment to the definition of sustainable forest management...Sustainable forest management is a process, and by implication, it is a commitment by the ITTO to install that process by 2000. It cannot be interpreted that by the year 2000, 100 per cent sustainability will be achieved...What is important and needed is that producer countries are seriously embarked on the path and process of sustainable forest management with tangible results visible, based on some newly adopted criteria and indicators for sustainable management of natural tropical forests.*'

Another contentious issue for tropical timber producers is timber certification, defined as 'a process which results in a written quality statement (a certificate) attesting the origin of the wood raw material, and its status and/or qualifications following validation by an independent third party.'

It involves certification on two fronts: in forest management practices and production of forest goods. The former involves the independent evaluation of the quality of forest management in the country of origin according to a set of pre-determined standards, known in Malaysia as Malaysian Criteria and Indicators (MC&I). The latter is a chain-of-custody or product certification, covering the supply chain

An MTC World Forestry Day poster
highlighting the tree-planting
campaign launched in 1997.

GETTING TOUGHER WITH ILLEGAL LOGGERS

In 1993, the National Forestry Act was amended to provide for tougher penalties for illegal logging. The amendment introduced a mandatory jail term of at least one year, with a maximum of twenty years upon conviction of illegal logging. There was also a staggering increase in the quantum of fines, with the ceiling being raised from RM10,000 (USD2,600) to RM500,000 (USD131,600). The amended Act also provides for the Director of Forestry to offer rewards to informers who help bring about seizures under the Act. An interesting feature of the Act is that the 'burden of proof' is on the accused, not on the prosecutor. The accused must prove that they were not involved in illegal activities. Thereby they are thought of as guilty until they can prove otherwise, a reverse of the normal 'innocent until proven guilty' premise.

27 suspected illegal loggers nabbed

Enforcement is carried out by Forestry Department officers who work together with the police and the army to curb illegal logging, forest encroachment and timber theft. These enforcement officers are empowered to stop and search forest vehicles, seize forest produce and search with or without a warrant.

The stringent measures contained in the amended Act appear to have taken effect. A recent WWF/World Bank study on Forest Law Enforcement in Peninsular Malaysia discloses that the incidence of forest crimes have shown a declining trend over the last several years and that there is no evidence to indicate that illegal logging is an organized crime.

The Forestry Department continues to enforce Malaysia's strict National Forestry Act against illegal loggers and traders.

of domestic and export markets—it tracks a forest product from the forest to its end-use, through the transportation, processing and distribution chain.

Studies conducted by the London Environmental Economics Centre, Greenpeace International and FAO all arrived at the conclusion that there is little linkage between commercial tropical forestry and tropical deforestation. This is because only six per cent of tropical hardwoods enter the international marketplace. Most tropical timber is used as fuelwood by local communities. Nonetheless, certification was adopted to meet demands of the marketplace, where consumer nations imposed boycotts, bans and trade restrictions on tropical timber imports, unless it is proven that the products came from sustainably managed forests.

Meanwhile, this drew attention to the issue of trade barriers, considered a violation of international agreements such as the General Agreement on Tariffs and Trade and the International Tropical Timber Agreement. In 1994, Denmark, The Netherlands and Germany used CITES to restrict international trade in tropical timber species such as *ramin (Gonystylus bancanus)* and *merbau (Intsia palembanica)*, only to be met with loud cries of 'Unfair trade practice!' from developing countries. Eventually, Malaysia successfully presented its case on *ramin* and *merbau* to CITES

Logs are inspected by officers at timber-checking stations en route to the mills.

The buttresses of a *merbau* (*Intsia palembanica*) tree. International trade in *merbau* was the subject of controversy in 1994 in CITES.

and won on the merit of their scientific data. This was a volatile period in the West-led green movement. The passion appears to have cooled and the closing years of the millennium were marked by more reason and less rage.

Notably, one of the loudest voices in the pro-certification lobby, the Dutch, decided to change direction and adopted a friendlier bilateral approach towards Malaysian timber imports. They collaborated on a pilot certification programme that culminated with the export of the first batch of 600 cubic metres of Malaysian audited tropical timber to The Netherlands in 1997. Called the Malaysia—Netherlands Cooperation Programme in Timber Certification, the project was led by the Malaysian Timber Industry Board (MTIB) and involved two phases of certification. It involved an independent third-party audit of forest management in the three states of Selangor, Pahang and Terengganu, which was followed up with chain-of-custody certification of the forest products. The Dutch partner in this exercise, the Keurhout Foundation, which consists of trade, timber and processing

FOREST MANAGEMENT REASSESSMENT IN TERENGGANU

Forest management assessment in Terengganu. (Above: left and right): Selecting the areas for assessment. Below left: In the field, locating the chosen assessment area. Below right: Assessing the slope of the road.

THE WONDERS OF WOOD

Wood is natural, organic, renewable, non-toxic, recyclable and biodegradable. A single piece of wood can be utilized many times over before it loses its properties. Being biodegradable, it will decompose on its own and return to the earth's cycle.

An article published in the *New Zealand Pine International* (1996 August/September issue), which is based on a study by Dr Peter Koch, estimates that global energy consumption will increase by between 25–141 million barrels of oil a day annually if non-renewable structural materials such as steel, aluminium, concrete, brick and plastics replace structural wood. In addition, atmospheric carbon dioxide will sky-rocket from 11–62 million tons annually.

Wood substitutes typically involve manufacturing processes that are not environmentally friendly. Turning a tree into sawntimber or veneer requires less energy and produces less pollution compared to the large amounts of electricity and heat needed to produce other materials. Emissions of carbon dioxide and other gases are also greater during the production of substitute building materials. Carbon dioxide emissions are three times greater when producing steel than sawntimber.

Wood grain images showing the beauty of some of the wide variety of Malaysian timbers.

Wood also helps conserve energy by serving as a good thermal insulator in construction, especially in window and door applications. It is natural and found in great quantities all over the world. And unlike fossil fuels like coal and oil, which take millions of years to replace, trees can be planted to yield timber within a lifetime.

1. Dark Red Meranti/Obar Suluk
2. Kapur
3. Merbau
4. Resak
5. Sepetir
6. Bintangor
7. Keruntum
8. Kembang Semangkok
9. Sentang
10. Balau/Selangan Batu
11. Kempas
12. Keruing
13. Chengal
14. Rubberwood
15. Rengas

1	2	3	4	5
6	7	8	9	10
11	12	13	14	15

Source: 100 Malaysian Timbers (MTIB)

industries and unions, verified that the declarations of sustainable forest management met the requirements of the Dutch government. The Foundation also manages the tracing system, developed by auditing firm Coopers and Lybrand and the Foundation Keuringsbureau Hout (SKH). In the case of imported timber, this tracing system tracks the passage of timber from the port of entry to the end-user.

This pilot study made use of the MC&I which was developed based on the ITTO Criteria and Indicators used to assess sustainable forestry management. To obtain chain-of-custody certification of their products, companies must apply to the Malaysian Timber Certification Council (MTCC) which operates the voluntary timber certification scheme to assure importers that Malaysian timber products are derived from sustainably managed forests.

'There are huge costs associated with the implementation of forest policies and regulations to ensure protection of conservation areas and proper enforcement of sustainable forest practices in tropical forests.'

– WORLD BANK

MTCC's phased approach to the implementation of timber certification involves the establishment of a national standard that is also compatible with those of the Forest Stewardship Council (FSC). The standard that is currently being used for assessing Forestry Management Units (FMUs) is the *Malaysian Criteria, Indicators, Activities and Standards of Performance for Forest Management Certification* (MC&I), which is based on the 1998 *ITTO Criteria and*

Indicators for Sustainable Management of Natural Tropical Forests. MC&I contains the key elements of forest mananagement assessment, taking into account the impact of forestry on the economy, society, the environment and species conservation.

The next phase involves establishing compatibililty between MC&I and the Principles and Criteria of the FSC, a body supported by WWF and other organizations. Work on the formulation of FSC-compatible MC&I is currently underway—the revised standard will eventually be submitted for FSC endorsement.

The Malaysian forest landscape has undergone some changes in recent years with the emergence of forest plantations and small agroforestry plots. And this trend is expected to continue given the findings of an MTC-commissioned survey in 1996 that disclosed that there is more than 2.82 million hectares of land that could be converted to productive forest plantations. Such land included tin tailings, former shifting cultivation areas and abandoned agricultural areas.

Forest plantations are more efficient in producing commercial timber than natural forests—the annual increment from plantations is between ten to twenty cubic metres per hectare per year compared to less than four cubic metres per hectare per year from natural forests. Furthermore, plantations are simpler to manage given their mono or duo species compared to the species diversity of natural forests. Plantations will thus serve as a strategy for the sustainable supply of timber, supplementing that derived from natural forests, which have the additional function of providing other benefits such as water supply, recreation and biodiversity. Most forest plantations have been developed by the public sector. In recognition of forest plantation as a strategic sector, the government offers tax incentives to encourage private investors to venture into forest plantation development.

In 2001, forest plantations accounted for 1.2 per cent of the 20.2 million hectares of forested land. In Peninsular Malaysia, forest plantations occupied 70,000 hectares that were planted mainly with species such as acacia (*Acacia mangium*), pine (*Pinus* spp.), *batai* (*Paraserianthes falcataria*) and *sentang* (*Azadirachta excelsa*).

The Worldwide Fund for Nature (WWF) is one of the world's most experienced independent conservation organizations, with an active global network in more than 90 countries.

OPPOSITE: The supply of timber from natural forests is supplemented by forest plantations.

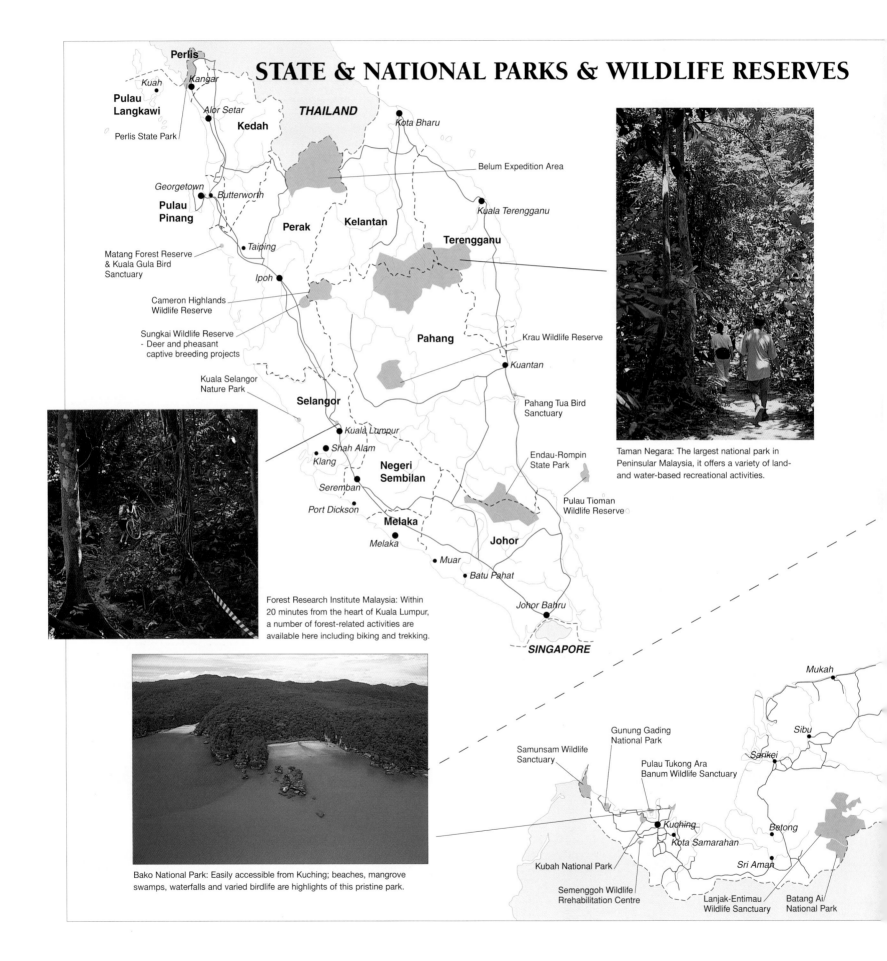

STATE & NATIONAL PARKS & WILDLIFE RESERVES

THAILAND

Perlis
Kuah
Kangar
Pulau Langkawi
Alor Setar
Kedah
Perlis State Park
Kota Bharu

Belum Expedition Area

Georgetown
Butterworth
Pulau Pinang
Perak
Kelantan
Kuala Terengganu
Terengganu

Matang Forest Reserve & Kuala Gula Bird Sanctuary
Taiping
Ipoh
Cameron Highlands Wildlife Reserve
Sungkai Wildlife Reserve - Deer and pheasant captive breeding projects

Pahang
Krau Wildlife Reserve

Kuantan

Kuala Selangor Nature Park
Pahang Tua Bird Sanctuary

Selangor
Kuala Lumpur
Shah Alam
Klang
Negeri Sembilan
Seremban
Port Dickson
Melaka
Melaka
Muar
Batu Pahat

Endau-Rompin State Park

Pulau Tioman Wildlife Reserve

Johor

Johor Bahru

SINGAPORE

Taman Negara: The largest national park in Peninsular Malaysia, it offers a variety of land- and water-based recreational activities.

Forest Research Institute Malaysia: Within 20 minutes from the heart of Kuala Lumpur, a number of forest-related activities are available here including biking and trekking.

Bako National Park: Easily accessible from Kuching; beaches, mangrove swamps, waterfalls and varied birdlife are highlights of this pristine park.

Mukah
Sibu
Sarikei
Gunung Gading National Park
Samunsam Wildlife Sanctuary
Pulau Tukong Ara Banum Wildlife Sanctuary
Kuching
Betong
Kota Samarahan
Kubah National Park
Sri Aman
Semenggoh Wildlife Rrehabilitation Centre
Lanjak-Entimau Wildlife Sanctuary
Batang Ai National Park

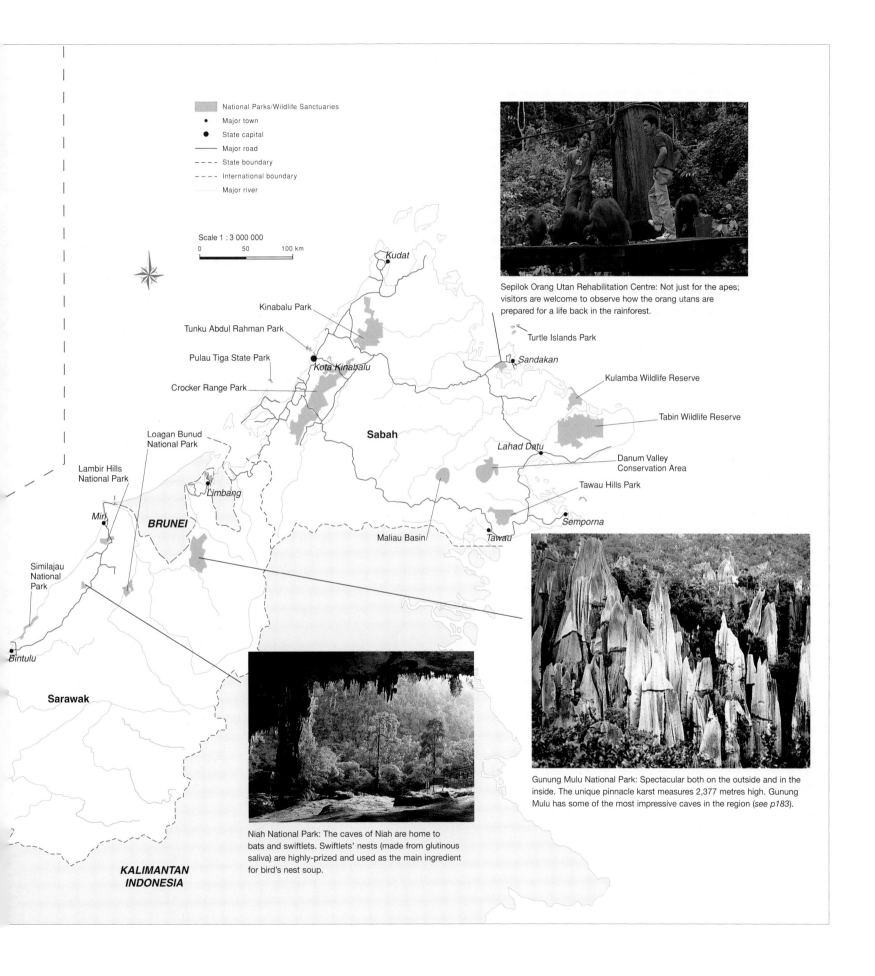

National Parks/Wildlife Sanctuaries
Major town
State capital
Major road
State boundary
International boundary
Major river

Scale 1 : 3 000 000
0   50   100 km

Kudat

Kinabalu Park

Tunku Abdul Rahman Park

Pulau Tiga State Park

Kota Kinabalu

Crocker Range Park

Sabah

Sandakan

Turtle Islands Park

Kulamba Wildlife Reserve

Tabin Wildlife Reserve

Lahad Datu

Danum Valley
Conservation Area

Tawau Hills Park

Loagan Bunud
National Park

Lambir Hills
National Park

Limbang

BRUNEI

Miri

Maliau Basin

Semporna

Tawau

Similajau
National
Park

Bintulu

Sarawak

KALIMANTAN
INDONESIA

Sepilok Orang Utan Rehabilitation Centre: Not just for the apes; visitors are welcome to observe how the orang utans are prepared for a life back in the rainforest.

Gunung Mulu National Park: Spectacular both on the outside and in the inside. The unique pinnacle karst measures 2,377 metres high. Gunung Mulu has some of the most impressive caves in the region (see p183).

Niah National Park: The caves of Niah are home to bats and swiftlets. Swiftlets' nests (made from glutinous saliva) are highly-prized and used as the main ingredient for bird's nest soup.

ABOVE: *Acacia mangium* is a fast-growing plantation species.

A rubber tree on the grounds of the Rubber Research Institute of Malaysia (RRIM) field station in Sungei Buloh. RRIM is the foremost rubber research institution in the world.

In Sabah, there are 150,000 hectares of forest plantations with 80 per cent planted with fast-growing species such as the acacia and *batai*, *yemane* (*Gmelina arborea*) and *Eucalyptus deglupta*. The 30,000 hectares of forest plantations in Sarawak consist mainly of *engkabang* (*Shorea* spp.) and acacia.

Another new facet of forestry is agroforestry, the marriage of agriculture and forestry, which was introduced under the Third National Agriculture Policy (NAP3, 1998–2010). In practice, it means that agricultural crops are grown between timber and non-timber species. Agroforestry is targeted mainly at smallholders and farmers, who are encouraged to plant commercial timber trees and cash crops on idle land and abandoned plantations. The diverse crop profile of agroforestry is regarded as a safer bet than monoculture. Apart from providing additional income and reducing the impact of price fluctuations of single cropping, agroforestry also results in greater space utilization. Instead of working vast areas, it uses existing agricultural land; timber trees can be planted together with other crops. Advocates also say integrating forest and agricultural species will improve the chemical and biological properties of soil, reduce weeding and control soil erosion and run-off. Trial plantations began in the mid–1990s, and these experiments included planting rattan (*Calamus* spp.) in rubber plantations, *sentang* (*Azadirachta excelsa*) in oil palm plantations, and *tongkat Ali* (*Eurycoma longifolia*) or *kacip Fatimah* (*Labisia pumila*) with teak (*Tectona grandis*).

WORLD HERITAGE LISTING FOR GUNUNG MULU AND KINABALU PARKS

Outstanding conservation icons that meet the four rigorous criteria for evaluation based on the Convention Concerning the Protection of the World Cultural and Natural Heritage adopted by UNESCO in 1972 are rewarded by being listed as World Heritage sites.

Gunung Mulu National Park and Kinabalu Park joined the ranks of World Heritage sites such as Mount Everest, Galápagos Islands, the Grand Canyon and the Great Barrier Reef in 2000. The 52,864-hectare Gunung Mulu site in Sarawak, which was gazetted as a national park in 1974, was described by the evaluation committee as the most studied tropical karst area in the world, important for both its high biodiversity and karst features. Mulu has a total of 17 vegetation zones with some 3,500 species of vascular plants and 109 species of palms. It is also home to the largest known cave

Gunung Mulu is one the largest limestone cave networks in the world; its spacious Sarawak Chamber can accommodate London's St Paul's Cathedral, while its Deer Cave, the largest cave in the world (over two kilometres long and 90 metres high and wide), can accommodate 47 jumbo jets.

chamber in the world, the 600 m x 415 m x 80 m Sarawak Chamber.

Kinabalu Park's listing was based on the park's rich and complex biodiversity, myriad of habitats, microhabitats and ecological niches, which have been the subject of research since 1852. The 75,370-hectare Sabah park that is centred around Mount Kinabalu, Southeast Asia's highest peak, is reputed to have the most remarkable assemblage of plants and animals in the world. Both Gunung Mulu National Park and Kinabalu Park are popular ecotourism destinations.

In addition to the natural forest cover, regeneration, rehabilitation, conversion, reafforestation and the use of modern technology have contributed to a greener Malaysia. There is a conscious effort to increase green cover. A total of 185,174 hectares of forested land in Peninsular Malaysia were gazetted as Permanent Forest Estate (PFE) in late 1997. In 1998, forests above 1,000 metres were gazetted as protected forests. In 2001, PFEs in Malaysia occupied 14.45 million hectares, consisting of 3.81 million hectares of protection forest and 10.64 million hectares of production forest.

Not only are Malaysia's national parks and sanctuaries a tribute to forest conservation and biodiversity, they also offer a host of forest adventures that has attracted ecotourists from all over the world. The rough and tough rainforest terrain has been the venue of numerous extreme sports such as the annual Sabah Adventure Challenge, which enjoys a reputation as a challenging and engaging race through some spectacular scenery. In its third year, the 2002 Challenge attracted 81 teams from Europe, America, Australia and Asia competing to win the gruelling three-day race that covered 180 kilometres in the Adventure category and 220 kilometres in the Extreme category. Teams run up to the summit of Mount Kinabalu, past the mist-shrouded montane forests of rhododendrons, wild orchids and pitcher plants, only to scramble onto mountain bikes for a roller-coaster ride downhill, across steep mountain

A bunch of oil palm fruits. Palm oil is a rich source of vitamin E.

LEFT: The beginning of the Sabah Adventure Challenge race.
Right: Preparing for the bike-leg of the race.

passes. One of the toughest parts of the race was the river rafting, where participants had to construct rafts from bamboo poles and row downstream along the river.

Other high adventures in the Malaysian rainforest include the annual Rainforest Challenge, regarded by some as the foremost 4x4 event in the world and the National Geographic Action Asia Challenge Series 2001–02. The former saw men and women pushing themselves and their machines to the limits as they drove through a torturous trail across the rainforest of Taman Negara in Peninsular Malaysia. Equally gruelling was the National Geographic endurance race in Pulau Pangkor. It tested competitors' ability in a variety of extreme sports: jungle trail running, mountain biking and kayaking.

For those more inclined to less extreme or gentler pursuits, the call of the wild can be fulfilled in a variety of other ways, from bird-watching and nature rambles to trekking, fishing and caving. Leading the pack of venues waiting to be explored is the 4,343-square-kilometre Taman Negara National Park, which houses Malaysia's oldest and largest tract of rainforest and is one of only 12 forests in the world with the most extensive biodiversity. It is a playground for mountain trekkers, anglers, birdwatchers and caving enthusiasts. Gunung Mulu National Park, which houses the world's largest

ABOVE: Building a bamboo raft for transportation down the river.

RIGHT: Competitors need to be extremely fit to compete in the gruelling race.

Competitors in the Sabah Adventure Challenge make their way across a rushing river to their next obstacle.

cave, has gained an enviable reputation for its spectacular limestone formations—primary pursuits for visitors are caving and trekking. The high altitude and montane vegetation of Kinabalu Park has the hearts of many racing as they scale the rocky faces to conquer Mount Kinabalu, Southeast Asia's highest peak. The wondrous beauty of montane vegetation, including chances of spotting *Rafflesia*, attracts many walkers to this scenic environment. Other popular old favourites are the hills of Gunung Ledang in Johor and Gunung Jerai in Kedah.

Malaysia's wilderness is fast becoming the 'goose that lays the golden egg', gilding national coffers with ecotourism ringgit. Mindful of the potential of ecotourism, the Ministry of Culture, Arts and Tourism has drawn up the National Ecotourism Plan, in collaboration with the Worldwide Fund for Nature Malaysia. A total of 52 sites, with 10 falling into the 'High Distinction' category, have been identified in the Plan, which contains guidelines on control measures to be taken for marine parks and islands, national parks and reserves, mangroves, recreational forests, mountains, caves, beaches, rivers, waterfalls and lakes. When fully implemented, the National Ecotourism Plan is expected to raise Malaysia's profile as a prime ecotourism destination, tapping the vast potential that exists in this rapidly growing travel industry. Endless possibilities exist outside the realm of mainstream tourism. Those found far away from familiar territory wait to be explored.

Kinabalu Park has a variety of terrain for adventurers to explore.

TIME NOW FOR BELUM

Belum Forest Reserve adjoins the Temenggor Forest Reserve in Upper Perak. Combined, these two reserves represent one of the largest remaining virgin forests in Malaysia. Proposals to gazette Belum as a State Park have previously been the subject of much debate between various parties. However, the approval of the Perak State Parks Enactment in 2001 should help pave the way for the the establishment of Belum State Park.

The forest is home to the Jahai, an Orang Asli tribe, who act as guides, taking visitors for wildlife viewing and fishing trips on the rivers that traverse the reserve. One of 29 Important Bird Areas (IBAs) in Malaysia, the reserve is also home to large numbers of elephant, tiger, rhinoceros, bear, tapir and deer.

THRILLS AT ENDAU-ROMPIN STATE PARK

Another newcomer in the state park scene, Endau Rompin State Park straddles the states of Pahang and Johor on the southern reaches of Peninsular Malaysia. It derives its name from two rivers: the Endau and the Rompin, which provide the reserve with its distinctive drawcard. Waterfalls abound and volcanic quartz crystal ignimbrite can be seen surfacing at many areas along the rapids of Sungai Endau.

The park is fast gaining a reputation as a place for shooting the rapids and jungle trekking, the latter best undertaken with Jakun Orang Asli guides. Endau-Rompin State Park enjoys a strong reputation as a wilderness park with unpolluted rivers and pristine lowland forests. The largest surviving population of Sumatran rhinoceros in Peninsular Malaysia is found in the park along with the tiger, the white-handed gibbon, wild boar, elephant, *binturong* (bear cat), hornbills, chirping drongos and the Great Argus pheasant.

PAYA INDAH WETLANDS: CONSERVATION CLOSE TO THE CAPITAL

Located 50 kilometres south of Kuala Lumpur, Paya Indah Wetlands is a 3,200-hectare wetland sanctuary consisting of natural peatswamp forests, rehabilitated degraded mining land, lakes and some measure of dry land. To protect the fragile wetlands, motorized transport is not allowed inside—instead, visitors have the option of walking, cycling or hiring a horse-drawn carriage to view the wonders of the wetlands. The sanctuary supports approximately 130 species of birds, 40 fish species and 26 species of mammals and reptiles. It is also home to protected species such as the grey-headed fish eagle, clouded leopard and more than 220 species of aquatic and terrestrial plants including some rare herbs. Developed in collaboration with Wetlands International, this conservation and rehabilitation project has, since its inception, in 1996 experienced a wildlife population increase of approximately 30 per cent.

Visitors can experience the beauty of the wetlands and birdlife from the water, in battery-operated boats or from boardwalks laid across the peatswamp. There are also picnic spots overlooking the scenic main lake and during the school holidays, nature camps are conducted for children between the ages of 10 and 17.

GIANTS OF THE DANUM VALLEY, SABAH

The Danum Valley Conservation Area on the western side of the Segama River about 70 kilometres east of Lahad Datu (the nearest town) occupies 438 square kilometres of virgin rainforest. It is home to the world's tallest rainforest trees, much taller than those found in the Amazon and equatorial Africa.

It is also one of the oldest and richest rainforests in the world, and was classified as Protection Forest Reserve (Class I) in May 1995. Put simply, this means that the valley is permanently protected. Fortunately, it is open to visitors, who can enjoy the splendour of rainforest giants from two canopy walkways that link three mighty *majau* and *tualang* trees. The L-shaped walkway is 27 metres above the ground and 107 metres long.

Nature lovers can also feast their eyes on the majesty of the seven-tiered waterfall and have the option of jungle trekking through thick undergrowth, muddy terrain and river crossings and to see an ancient Dusun burial site. Over 235 bird species have been recorded at Danum and many mammals can be seen here including squirrels, tree-shrews, civets, deer, elephant, Sumatran rhinoceros, clouded leopard, bearded pig, orang utan and the Western tarsier.

Accommodation in chalets modelled after traditional Kadazan-Dusun homes is offered at the Borneo Rainforest Lodge. Overnight camping trips to the remote Maliau Basin can also be arranged from Danum.

THE LOST WORLD OF THE MALIAU BASIN, SABAH

The Maliau Basin Conservation Area of 390 square kilometres is a pristine region located in the remote south central area of Sabah. This isolated, elevated saucer-shaped 25-kilometre diameter basin is surrounded by sheer escarpment, which forms an impregnable barrier to human settlement. To date, there is little evidence of human habitation save some items left behind by nomadic tribes.

The isolation of this basin has created a unique micro-habitat that has been conducive for the evolution of a few distinctly different species. To date, much of this 'lost world' has been the object of curiosity for scientists, seeking to study its special flora and fauna. The state government is formulating a comprehensive management plan to improve public access and establish

ecotourism projects, with a view to attaining World Heritage Status for this piece of wilderness. It was upgraded to a Protection Forest Reserve (Class I) in 1997 and the conservation area size was extended to its present size of 588.4 square kilometres, encompassing the basin itself and forested land to the north and east of the basin rim. Visitors to Maliau Basin Conservation Area are welcome, but access is strictly controlled and permission to enter must be obtained from Yayasan Sabah (Sabah Foundation). Camping is the only accommodation available.

CHAPTER EIGHT

FORESTS FOR THE FUTURE

For a greater part of the last millennium, forests were valued mainly for their products. Forest dwellers and rural communities felled trees for shifting agriculture and for wood and non-wood products that were used at home or sold to traders. Large companies, meanwhile, engaged in large-scale forestry that resulted in the removal of prized timber for profit. Rapid urbanization, industrialization, population expansion, agriculture, war and mining exacerbated the situation, worsening the state of forests. The nett result: the disappearance of vast tracts of biologically rich virgin forests in many countries with a forest heritage.

A World Wildlife Fund International report published in May 1994 entitled *'The Status of Old-growth and Ancient Semi-natural Forests in Western Europe'* observed that virgin temperate forests once covered 95 per cent of Western Europe. Today, forests cover about one third of Western Europe, with 0.2 per cent left as virgin forest. Deforestation there was caused mainly by extensive agriculture and industrialization. But lessons have been learnt and forestry today involves sustainable practices aimed at perpetuating forest life albeit secondary stands.

It is an altogether different story in Asia and Africa, where deforestation continues to loom large till this day, no thanks to grinding poverty. A 1995 Asian Development Bank report says that deforestation in Asia and Africa is driven by poverty, with local communities eking a living by felling trees for fuelwood and clearing the forest to plant food crops. Trees were said to be removed at an alarming rate of 700 million cubic metres a year, which is seven times greater than the annual harvest of commercial loggers. The United Nations' Food and Agricultural Organization (FAO) says that there is only one solution in sight—poverty eradication. And herein lies the future of most tropical forests of the world.

Meanwhile, commercial logging is increasingly built around sustainable forest management that places a premium on sustained-yield management practices to ensure the existence of forests in perpetuity for the long-term survival of forest products industries. Sustainable Forest Management (SFM) in its current form, however, is also in the throes of change. It is undergoing a paradigm shift that takes it

Sprigs of the *merbau* (*Intsia palembanica*) have 1–4 pairs of pinnate leaves.

OPPOSITE: Plants growing on river banks prevent soil erosion, one of the many invaluable functions of the forest.

Lakes and rivers are an important source of food and water to local communities.

one step up the ladder of forest management—instead of being primarily focused on sustainable timber yields, SFM has started to embrace multi-resource forest management practices involving the optimum production of several interdependent forest goods and services.

Forest resources extend beyond timber. They include non-wood products such as plants and animals for food and medicine, water, rattan, bamboo, dyes and resins. Forest services relate to recreation and aesthetics that form the basis of their role as ecotourism destinations. In addition, forests perform a wide range of invaluable functions that are often taken for granted. Indeed, forests play a critical role as watersheds, pollution control agents and in the prevention of soil erosion and land degradation. These wondrous workings of the forest have to be protected to avoid disasters such as landslides, drought, famine, diseases and a host of other attendant ills that can wreak havoc on all life forms.

CONSTRUCTING A WETLANDS IN THE CITY

Located in the heart of Putrajaya, the Federal Government Administrative Centre of Malaysia, the 197–hectare Putrajaya Wetlands represent a milestone in Malaysia's environmental programme. Completed in 1998, it is one of the largest man-made freshwater wetlands in the tropics. Straddling Sungai Chua and Sungai Bisa, it consists of a series of 24 wetland cells that were constructed to replicate a wetlands environment.

Water from these rivers and their tributaries flow through wetland cells planted with plant species that remove impurities contained in the flowing water. The water is filtered as it progresses through the cells before it empties into the lake, which is used for recreation such as wind surfing, boating and fishing.

The wetlands have attracted wildlife, especially birds, including the migratory cattle egret (*Bubulcus ibis*). A park has been built around the wetlands, for recreation as well as research and education. On the grounds is Nature Interpretation—a resource centre for tropical wetlands. Guided tours to the wetlands via boardwalks are also available.

Putrajaya Wetlands is divided into six wetlands containing a series of 24 cells which are separated by bunds. The cells filter the river water before it is released into the city's main lake. Cells are stocked with fish to balance the ecosystem.

In the closing years of the last millennium, there was increased recognition of these environmental, conservational and protective roles of forests. Indeed, it has been accepted that the burden of forest manangement and conservation should be equitably shared by the international community. This was loudly acknowledged by the 172 countries that participated in UNCED (Earth Summit) in 1992 in Rio de Janeiro (*see p16*). Representatives of governments, private agencies and non-governmental organizations, who were brought together for the first time to work on saving the environment, attended the summit and in a much-needed show of unity, many nations adopted Agenda 21 (*see pp18, 21*), the action plan that was in essence the catch phrase of environmentalists a decade ago—'Think Global, Act Local'—to chart the course of action for the 21st century.

Waterfalls are ideal recreation areas for the local population and tourists.

The Earth Summit in Rio was a turning point for Malaysia, which gained recognition as a responsible manager of tropical forests. It was seen and heard as the voice of reason representing the interests of the Group of 77 developing countries (G77). The high point came when Malaysia negotiated on behalf of the G77 and China, the adoption of the document: *'Non-Legally Binding Authoritative Statement of Principles for a Global Consensus on the Management, Conservation and Sustainable Development of all Types of Forests'* (Forest Principles).

During the Earth Summit, Malaysia also sealed its commitment to a greener world, with the Prime Minister, Dato' Seri Dr Mahathir Mohamad pledging: *'Malaysia would like to propose to the world community a comprehensive environmentally beneficial programme involving the greening of the world. As a first step, we call upon the global community to target at least 30 per cent of the Earth's terrestrial area to be greened by the year 2000. The world now has 27.6 per cent of its forests under forest cover and we need only to increase this by 2.4 per cent over the next eight years. This is clearly not an unreasonable target. All nations must set national greening targets and those which have no suitable land must contribute adequate funds to developing countries with available land.*

As for Malaysia, I wish to announce that the Government of Malaysia undertakes to ensure that at least 50 per cent of our land will remain permanently under forest cover.'

INSET: Currently 58 per cent of Malaysia remains under forest cover.

LANJAK-ENTIMAU/BENTUANG-KARIMUN TRANSBOUNDARY BIODIVERSITY CONSERVATION AREA

Transboundary forestry projects are joint regional efforts to sustainably manage invaluable tracts of forested land. One such project is the ITTO-initiated collaboration on biodiversity conservation between the Lanjak-Entimau Wildlife Sanctuary in southwestern Sarawak, Malaysia and the Bentuang-Karimun National Park (BKNP) in West Kalimantan, Indonesia. With a combined area of almost one million hectares, this contiguous area forms one of the world's largest transboundary biodiversity reserves in the tropical rainforest.

These species-rich forests have been identified as a centre for conservation, research and training. On both sides of the border, scientific biodiversity inventories are being compiled and forestry staff trained to raise the level of technical expertise for the long-term development of biodiversity-based resources. There is also special emphasis

The biotechnology industry will benefit from research and development efforts in the species-rich rainforests of Malaysia and Indonesia.

on the development of gene banks for economically important timber species, cultivation of non-timber forest products

such as rattan and the cultivation of medicinal plants by communities. Field surveys in Lanjak-Entimau/Bentuang-Karimun have led to the identification of more than 1,000 tree species exceeding ten centimetres in diameter, making the area among the most floristically rich sites studied in Borneo. It also contains an abundance of valuable timber species, with research teams designating several areas as gene banks or seed sources for the future.

Botanical surveys undertaken with the help of indigenous communities have led to the identification of 140 species of plants for traditional medicine and at least 114 varieties of wild fruits and vegetables consumed as food. Across the border in BKNP, working with local communities has shed light on the existence of an extensive body of indigenous knowledge on agricultural practices, usage of non-wood products and ethnobiology.

Malaysia's post-Rio greening programme focuses on both forest products and services. Total forested area covers 62 per cent of the total land today; of this, 71.5 per cent or 14.45 million hectares have been designated as Permanent Forest Estates and 19.4 per cent or 3.92 million hectares as Conversion Forests. Together, they provide a stable supply of forest products for use by local communities, industries and for export. Another 9.1 per cent or 1.83 million hectares have been classified as national parks for recreation as well as to safeguard forest functions such as water resource management, biodiversity conservation, soil enrichment and the mitigation of soil erosion and floods.

In addition, a network of 135 Virgin Jungle Reserves (VJR) occupying 113,444 hectares has been established. These serve as permanent nature reserves and natural arboreta for ecological and botanical research. These *in situ* conservation sites also serve as control areas in comparative studies between silviculturally treated forests and undisturbed forests. There are also plans to extend the VJR network to ensure the full representation of forest types found in Malaysia. Equally important, especially for threatened plant species and as a source of germplasm, are *ex situ*

Covering a 32-hectare area, this Virgin Jungle Reserve in the mangroves of Pulau Kecil, Perak, was set up in 1971.

conservation sites established in botanical gardens, zoological parks, arboreta, research institutions, government agencies and universities. There has also been extensive urban greening, which was boosted with the launch of a nationwide tree-planting campaign in 1997. The campaign target is to plant 20 million trees by the year 2020 and to date, tree plantings have exceeded annual targets.

Under the 7th Malaysia Plan (1996-2000), RM200 million (USD80 million) was allocated for landscaping government land, open areas, roadsides, river banks and industrial zones bordering residential areas. The Forest Research Institute Malaysia (FRIM) recommended 10 species for this purpose: *sentang* (*Azadirachta excelsa*), *janda merana* (*Salix babylonica*), *pulai* (*Alstonia angustiloba*), *kayu manis* (*Cinnamomum zeylanicum*), *simpoh* (*Dillenia* sp.), *kelat jambu laut* (*Eugenia grandis*), *kasai daun kecil* (*Pometia pinnata*), *kelumpang* (*Sterculia parviflora*), *takoma* (*Tabebuia pentaphylla*) and *merawan siput jantan* (*Hopea odorata*). Apart from their aesthetic value, these species also perform useful services, namely mitigating air pollution and soil erosion. Landscaping has also become a vital component of public and private real estate development projects. The prestigious Kuala Lumpur City Centre (KLCC) with its landmark Petronas Twin Towers had a landscaping budget of RM60 million (USD15.8 million) to create a

Malaysians of all ages participate in tree-planting campaigns across the country.

Urban greening: KLCC Park, which adjoins the Petronas Twin Towers, is the most recent 'green' addition to the Malaysian capital, which features several other parks and gardens.

BIO VALLEY

Malaysia's rich forest and agricultural heritage will form the basis of the country's biotechnology industries and services, which will be clustered around Bio Valley in the Multimedia Super Corridor, Malaysia's 15 kilometre by 50 kilometre superhighway that is to be the test bed for new technologies. The Bio Valley vision is to integrate bio-technology with Information Technology (IT) to spearhead the growth of the biotechnology industry.

The Bio Valley project will include a business development directorate and three new research institutions specializing in neutaceuticals, pharmaceuticals, agri-biotechnology, molecular biology and genomics and will be undertaken in collaboration with existing universities in the Klang Valley. The seeds for the project were sown when the government set up a

The focus on biotechnology research and development is expected to boost Malaysia's non-wood industries such as herbal medicine, pharmaceuticals and agro-based industries.

Biotechnology Partnership Programme with the Massachusetts Institute of Technology (MIT) in 1999. The programme was initiated to encourage collaboration between MIT and Malaysia-based researchers and to train a group of 160 Malaysian scientists.

So far, the programme has produced two patent applications—one for an anti-cancer agent drug and another for a com-pound found in a local plant traditionally used as an aphrodisiac. In addition, more than 8,000 oil palm genes and ten pre-viously unknown chemical compounds have been identified from Malaysian medicinal plants.

Biotechnology is set to be the path forward for Malaysia, with the Bio Valley the hub of a multi-billion ringgit industry, housing 50 home-grown biotechnology companies and creating thousands of jobs.

'Only through a fundamental respect for nature and a collaborative effort to manage our natural resources and share the planet with all living species can we preserve the Earth's generous natural riches for future generations.'

– KLAUS TOEPFLER, EXECUTIVE DIRECTOR UNITED NATIONS ENVIRONMENT PROGRAMME 12 SEPTEMBER 2000 (IN WELCOMING THE MILLENNIUM SUMMIT DECLARATION AT UN HEADQUARTERS IN NEW YORK)

green lung in the heart of the capital city. Equally impressive is the landscape at the Kuala Lumpur International Airport, whose theme is 'The Airport in A Forest & Forest in the Airport.' The city of Putrajaya, the Federal Government Administrative Centre of Malaysia, has been built around the theme, 'A Garden City, An Intelligent City'.

Forests know no borders and the issue of protecting shared forest resources was resolved by establishing regional arrangements particularly with ASEAN neighbours such as Thailand and Indonesia with whom Malaysia embarked on transboundary projects to conserve biologically rich tracts of rainforest. SFM research and development has taken top priority with additional funds allocated to FRIM for projects involving forest management, conservation and production in line with timber certification requirements. In addition, Malaysia has collaborated with global organizations such as the ITTO, foreign agencies such as DANCED, JICA and GTZ, to acquire new skills and technologies, and non governmental organizations such as the Asian Wetlands Bureau, Worldwide Fund for Nature and, on a more local level, with the Malaysian Nature Society to collaborate on conservation projects.

All these steps have been the foundation of the 8th Malaysia Plan (2001–2005). The focus is on multiple resource management to ensure a healthy environment where the air and water is clean, food is secure and produced with minimal use of chemicals, towns and cities are unpolluted and natural habitats and resources are conserved to safeguard

Malaysia's rich biodiversity. A National Biodiversity Policy is already in place that provides for the involvement of the Ministries of Primary Industries and Agriculture, the Departments of Wildlife and National Parks and Fisheries. Among others, it includes strategies to conserve biological diversity and the use of biological resources. Meanwhile, environmentally friendly logging practices are to be expanded with a further refinement of reduced impact logging technologies. Timber certification is encouraged with the establishment of the Malaysian Timber Certification Council (MTCC), which will also collaborate with other timber certification bodies. However, government initiatives will come to nought without public cooperation. Environmental awareness and education programmes that began in the 1980s will continue to draw upon the resources of the public and private sector and non-governmental organizations to communicate the environmental concerns of the day.

The 'Forest in the Airport' can be clearly seen at the departure terminal of Kuala Lumpur International Airport.

While everyone agrees that SFM is of paramount importance in striking a balance between environmental concerns and economic needs, there are still several issues that need to be resolved worldwide. While the concept of SFM is readily accepted, its practice is often hamstrung by the shortage of funds and scientific, technological and professional staff as well as institutional capacities to fully realize its benefits. This has proven to be one of the biggest challenges for forest managers in developing countries.

Another is the economic valuation of forests, which is currently based on monetary costs of extraction and distribution of timber, without factoring in the environmental

Oil palm plantations contribute towards increasing the green cover of the country.

and social costs. This means that there is little incentive to safeguard the environment, which has suffered as a result. It is thus imperative that national forestry policies factor in the cost of forest depletion into their national accounting system.

Then there is the question of choices to be made. Food security or forest sustainability? Short-term measures or long-term benefits? There is intense pressure to clear forests for agriculture to feed the world's growing population. While it is agreed that forests have to be converted for agriculture, opinion is divided over the extent of the forest. Some believe that the answer lies in biotechnology that will spur a green revolution to increase farm yields. The FAO, on the other hand, estimates that an additional 50 million hectares of tropical forests in developing nations may have to be converted for agriculture by the year 2010. Hence, deforestation is likely to continue in many developing countries, at least in the short-term.

The conservation of biological diversity in forest ecosystems also requires some hard decisions. Tropical rainforests are fragile ecosystems that disintegrate easily with repeated human intervention. Given the need to strike a balance between economic and environmental needs, choices have to be made to prioritize some habitats and species over others based on current knowledge. Biological diversity is also the cornerstone of the biotechnology industry, which in turn raises the issue of intellectual property rights and patents of products derived from forest genetic resources.

Lata Bukit Hijau in Baling, Kedah, a popular destination for forest recreation.

There is a need to establish a mechanism for the equitable sharing of benefits arising from the commercial utilization of genetic resources with the country of their origin, especially with regard to compensation payments to indigenous communities whose knowledge and expertise were utilized to develop these biotechnology products.

International trade in tropical forest products also needs further refinement to establish more equitable systems that meet the needs of both consumers and producers. The current system of eco-labelling and the Convention on International Trade in Endangered Species of Wild Fauna and Flora (CITES) criteria for listing endangered plants and animals begs the question whether they are non-tariff barriers imposed by consumers on developing countries. Tropical timber producers also tend to find themselves in a vicious cycle of restricted market access which, in turn, results in low returns on their investment in SFM practices.

Another contentious issue is carbon-trading between developed and developing countries. Based on the noble idea of reducing global warming, carbon-trading involves industrialized countries investing in clean emission-

Taiping Lake Gardens, one of the oldest gardens in Malaysia, was built around abandoned tin mines. It is well known for its majestic raintrees, ferns and orchids.

reducing projects in developing countries to earn credits to meet their own greenhouse gas targets set by the United Nations Framework Convention on Climate Change (*see p16*). Developing countries in turn acquire private capital investment and advanced technology. But there is a catch. Carbon-trading is a market-based instrument, with the potential for price wars among countries bidding for projects. This, in turn, may result in the investors earning their carbon credits by dumping sub-optimum technologies on unsuspecting developing countries. To avert the negative effects of carbon-trading, a fixed price mechanism is being proposed by some developing countries.

Ten years after the Rio Summit, the representatives of government, business, industry and civil society assembled once again at the World Summit on Sustainable Development (Rio+10) in Johannesburg, South Africa between 26 August and 4 September 2002. The agenda of this summit was to discuss and debate several of the aforementioned issues when charting the next course of action for the sustainable development of all nations on Planet Earth.

Malaysia, which embarked on its journey to Rio+10 with fervour, was able to attend the summit with its head held high given its unwavering commitment to the Forest Principles and Agenda 21. Today, it has in place not only several systems and processes for sustainable development, but has also been commended for several efforts, notably forestry management. A strong SFM foundation has been laid and it will pave the way for further progress as the country presses ahead for greater environmental vigilance both in its own backyard and around the world.

Plants are often featured on Malaysian postage stamps. Top to bottom: *Bungor* (*Lagerstroemia floribunda*), *perah* (*Elateriospermum tapos*), *kapur* (*Dryobalanops aromatica*), *tembusu padang* (*Fagraea fragrans*).

Bibliography

Allen, Betty Molesworth (1975), *Common Malaysian Fruits*, Malaysia: Longman.

Bock, Carl (1991), *The Head-Hunters of Borneo*, Singapore: Oxford University Press.

Bourke, William M. (2000), *Escape to the Great Outdoors of West Malaysia*, Malaysia: High Adventure Publishing.

Braack, L. E. O. *Fascinating Insects of Southeast Asia*, Singapore: Times Editions.

Brooke, Margaret (1989), *My Life in Sarawak,* Singapore: Oxford University Press.

Chin, H. F. (1977), *Malaysian Flowers in Colour*, Kuala Lumpur: Tropical Press.

Chin, H. F. and Enoch I. C. (1995), *Malaysian Trees in Colour*, Kuala Lumpur: Tropical Press.

Chin, H. F and Yong, H. S. (1980), *Malaysian Fruits in Colour*, Kuala Lumpur: Tropical Press.

Chin, Lucas and Mashman, Valerie (1991), *Sarawak, Cultural Legacy,* Malaysia: Society Atelier Sarawak.

Davison, G.W. H. and Chew Yen Fook (1995), A *Photographic Guide to Birds of Peninsular Malaysia and Singapore*, London: New Holland.

Davison, G.W. H. and Chew Yen Fook (1996), A *Photographic Guide to Birds of Borneo*, London: New Holland.

Earl of Cranbrook and Edwards, David S. (1994), *A Tropical Rainforest: The nature of biodiversity in Borneo at Belalong, Brunei*, Singapore: Sun Tree Publishing and The Royal Geographical Society, London.

Francis, Charles M. (1995), *Pocket Guide to the Birds of Borneo*, Malaysia: Sabah Society and WWF Malaysia.

Groombridge, Brian (ed.) (1992), *Global Biodiversity, Status of the Earth's Living Resources*, London: Chapman and Hall.

Harrison, Tom (1990), *World Within, A Borneo Story*, Singapore: Oxford University Press.

Hornaday, William T (1993), *The Experiences of a Hunter and Naturalist in the Malay Peninsula and Borneo*, Kuala Lumpur: Oxford University Press.

Innes, Emily (1993), *The Chersonese with the Gilding Off*, Kuala Lumpur: Oxford University Press.

Jones, David T. (1993), *Flora of Malaysia Illustrated*, Kuala Lumpur: Oxford University Press.

King, Victor T (1993), *The Peoples of Borneo*, Oxford: Blackwell.

Malaysian Timber Council, (1995–2001) *Malaysia Timber Bulletins*: Kuala Lumpur: Malaysian Timber Council.

Mastaller, Michael (1997), *Mangroves, The Forgotten Forest Between Land and Sea*, Kuala Lumpur: Tropical Press.

Nicholas, Colin and Singh, Raajen (eds.) (1996), *Indigenous Peoples of Asia, Many Peoples, One Struggle*, Bangkok: Asia Indigenous Peoples Pact.

Nilsson, Nils-Erik (ed.) (1990), *The Forests*, Sweden: SNA Publishing.

Payne, Junaidi and Cubbit, Gerald, (1990), *Wild Malaysia, The wildlife and scenery of Peninsular Malaysia, Sarawak and Sabah*, United Kingdom: New Holland Publishers.

Payne, Junaidi, Cubbit, Gerald, Lau, Dennis, (1994), *This is Borneo*, United Kingdom: New Holland.

Payne, Junaidi, Francis, Charles, M. Philipps, Karen, (1985), *A Field Guide to the Mammals of Borneo*, Malaysia: The Sabah Society and WWF Malaysia.

Polunin, Ivan (1988), *Plants and Flowers of Malaysia*, Singapore: Times Editions.

Poore, Duncan (1989), *No Timber Without Trees, Sustainability in the Tropical Forest*, London: Earthscan Publications.

Prescott-Allen, Robert (1991), *Caring for the Earth, A Strategy for Sustainable Living*, Switzerland: World Conservation Union, United Nations Environment Programme, World Wide Fund For Nature.

Roth, Henry Ling (1980), *The Natives of Sarawak and British North Borneo*, Kuala Lumpur: University of Malaya Press.

Rubeli, Ken (1994), *Tropical Rain Forest in South-East Asia – A Pictorial Journey*, Kuala Lumpur: Tropical Press.

Salam Abdullah, A. (1995), *Poisonous Plants of Malaysia*, Kuala Lumpur: Tropical Press.

Sani, Sham (ed.) (1998), *Volume 1 – Environment, Encyclopedia of Malaysia*, Malaysia: Archipelago Press.

Sharp, Ilsa and Compost, Alain (1994), *Green Indonesia, Tropical Forest Encounters*, Kuala Lumpur: Oxford University Press.

Soepadmo, E. (ed.) (1998), *Volume 2 – Plants, Encyclopedia of Malaysia*, Malaysia: Archipelago Press.

Stone, David (1994), *Tanah Air: Indonesia's Biodiversity*, Singapore: Archipelago Press.

Tan Teck Koon (1990), *A Guide to Tropical Fungi*, Singapore: Singapore Science Centre.

Taylor, Barbara (1996), *Animal Homes*, London: Dorling Kindersley.

Tweedie, M. W. F. (1989), *Common Birds of the Malay Peninsula*, Malaysia: Longman.

Tweedie, M. W. F. (1978), *Mammals of Malaysia*, Malaysia: Longman.

Tweedie, M. W. F. and Harrison, J. L. (1988), *Malayan Animal Life*, Malaysia: Longman.

Veevers-Carter, W. (1984), *Riches of the Rain Forest*, Singapore: Oxford University Press.

William Warren (1996), *Tropical Flowers of Malaysia and Singapore*, Singapore: Periplus Editions.

Wong, K. M. (1995), *The Bamboos of Peninsular Malaysia*, Malaysia: Forest Research Institute of Malaysia.

Wyatt-Smith, J. and Kochummen, K. M. (1979), *Pocket Check List of Timber Trees*, Malaysia: Forest Department, Peninsular Malaysia.

Yong Hoi Sen (ed.) (1998), *Volume 3 – Animals, Encyclopedia of Malaysia*, Malaysia: Archipelago Press.

Index